T0193197

Whispers
from
the Light

GARY BORIERO

BALBOA.
PRESS
A DIVISION OF HAY HOUSE

Scripture taken from the King James Version of the Bible.

Balboa Press books may be ordered through booksellers or by contacting:

Balboa Press
A Division of Hay House
1663 Liberty Drive
Bloomington, IN 47403
www.balboapress.com
1 (877) 407-4847

Because of the dynamic nature of the Internet, any web addresses or links contained in this book may have changed since publication and may no longer be valid. The views expressed in this work are solely those of the author and do not necessarily reflect the views of the publisher, and the publisher hereby disclaims any responsibility for them.

The author of this book does not dispense medical advice or prescribe the use of any technique as a form of treatment for physical, emotional, or medical problems without the advice of a physician, either directly or indirectly. The intent of the author is only to offer information of a general nature to help you in your quest for emotional and spiritual well-being. In the event you use any of the information in this book for yourself, which is your constitutional right, the author and the publisher assume no responsibility for your actions.

Any people depicted in stock imagery provided by Thinkstock are models, and such images are being used for illustrative purposes only. Certain stock imagery © Thinkstock.

Print information available on the last page.

ISBN: 978-1-5043-7718-8 (sc)
ISBN: 978-1-5043-7720-1 (hc)
ISBN: 978-1-5043-7719-5 (e)

Library of Congress Control Number: 2017904280

Balboa Press rev. date: 04/24/2017

In memory of my father Lucian Boriero for giving me life
and teaching me it's most precious
lesson, unconditional love – G.B.

Acknowledgements

To Steve Azer, the reason I manifest my dreams.

To Gloria Baker, the warmest hug and loving heart. By destiny we met. Thank you for believing in me.

To Natasha Josefowitz for your relentless love, support and push for me to write this book and for the magical visits every week.

To Sufian Chaudhary, you are a Master; by knowing you I have been activated into a world of living, breathing, unconditional love. Thank you for awakening the memories and connection to what I have always known in my heart. You are my brother for eternity.

To my mother Ruth Corning, the unshakable love for all of your children and family and friends is an inspiration.

To Wayne Dyer, for taking some of the world's greatest messages and putting them into language we can all understand. You are my hero and the inspiration for writing this book.

To Oprah, for showing me how to create the life I want through mediation and dynamic volition. It all started with you. Thank you for showing me the way.

To everyone holding this book; believe that you are the spark of creation and conduit of love that holds us together as one.

Prologue

We begin our journey in life on a little blue speck called earth located in the middle of an infinite universe of planets, stars and the unknown. If we think about it long or hard enough, it is amazing that we exist at all. Yet against the odds, we are alive and following a path that was designed and orchestrated just for us. If we share our stories, we will find we are more connected than we ever imagined. Even though I never set out to share mine, it became apparent after many long conversations with a friend that it was my destiny. Once the powerful wheels were set in motion, I couldn't stop writing. This book is about the incredible experiences that have awakened my consciousness and given me unshakable proof there is more to our existence than meets the eye. Miracles are everywhere and the connection we share is magically shown to us each and every day if we only pay attention to the signs.

It seems to me we do not become enlightened together, we become enlightened alone. I have taken bits and pieces of books, teachings and experiences to arrive where I AM at today. I believe that our journey is one of self-realization. We truly cannot completely understand another's journey. I may resonate with someone else's, but each is entirely unique. I have heard it said many times that religion is somebody else's experience of God. I ask the question, what is mine? I say, be yourself, be true to your own journey and beliefs. Explore and find the paths that lead to the truths that resonate in your head and heart. Rest assured that there is something magical and wonderful happening at the core of your existence. Create the essential habit of meditation every day and you will find your mind opening like a flower to the sun. You will begin to experience an elevation of your soul and consciousness each and everyday if you work at it. Don't be afraid to talk about your truth. Unless you are willing to share your truth, you won't ever connect to like souls. I believe that while we evolve spiritually alone, we are not meant to be alone. We need each other physically and emotionally. We are meant to hold and be held, love and be loved in return. We are meant to share our life, our thoughts and dreams and maybe experience one of the most powerful things in creation, creation itself.

As you read through these pages I AM hopeful of one thing, you will find you are not alone. Even in your most personal thoughts, there are others just like you.

Truth

I believe in reincarnation. Reincarnation is the belief that the soul survives death and comes back as another living being based on its Karmic inheritance. In the law of Karma everything we do in life has a consequence. Every time we chose an action, there is a consequence to that action. In the bible, it is the principle that we reap what we sow. If we are harmful to others, then harm will come to us. If we are loving and kind, then in return we will receive an abundance of love and kindness. When it comes to concepts, beliefs and paths we must all find our way somehow, but with so many options, how does one choose? I learned very young that when my head and my heart are in total alignment, it is truth. This alignment has rarely steered me in the wrong direction.

Family

Why we return to body and choose our family is fuzzy at first since we rarely know the reasons until later in life as lessons unfold. But if we examine closely, we begin to see the perfect combination of experiences needed to point us in the direction of what I believe we came here to learn, unconditional love.

I came into this world from the seemingly unlikely coupling of an Italian immigrant father and a Midwestern farmer's daughter. My dad grew up in a war-torn Italy and survived the Nazi work camps. He was proud to come to America and fight in the Korean War. This is how he earned his U.S. citizenship. Mom, the daughter of an affluent farmer and landowner, lived a sheltered idyllic life. She was young, naïve and wanted to have fun and dad was fun. The two of them met at a party, fell madly in love and were married much to the displeasure of mom's family. Prejudice against Italians was strong in those days so shortly thereafter they moved out West to California where tolerance was greater. It was several years after moving to Burbank that my soul rejoined its karmic family. The unlikely coupling became very likely as the years went by and the karmic ties that bound us were revealed.

The Four Gifts

My first memory in this life was lying in a bassinette at the base of the family Christmas tree fascinated by the twinkling lights, the smell of pine and calming sound of music in the air. This was just days after I was born. The first time I shared this memory with my mom she didn't believe me, "Really? You couldn't possibly remember that." She told me that shortly after bringing me home from the hospital she laid me under the Christmas tree for hours at a time. I never fussed, only stared at the Christmas lights and smiled. A photographic memory was the first gift I was given. I have always been able to recount my life like a movie in vivid detail.

While not herself from a religious family, during the first years of life my mom felt it was important to take us to church. Since dad was excommunicated for marrying outside of the Catholic faith, mom decided to raise us Methodist. Dad didn't want to raise us Catholic as he had a bad taste in his mouth from his experiences in Italy during the war. Once, a priest upset with his behavior in school took his bible and tore out a page that illustrated his family tree for generations and burned it in front of him. He told me it was the only record he had of our ancestors and it was gone forever.

I never felt the presence of God at church or resonated with religion. However, it was at Sunday services that I first witnessed something I never thought was different until much later in life. As I watched the minister intently giving his sermon, I could see colors emanating from his hands and body like heat waves appear rising from asphalt on a hot summer day. Trails of green, white and yellow emanated from his hands, shoulders and head as he moved around the pulpit. When he spoke passionately, the color would change to red like fire. The second gift, though I didn't know it then, was my first glimpse of energy and auras. Particles formed together to create waves of color that I would later learn were the vehicle to memories, thoughts and experiences of complete strangers. I lived my childhood in silence having the unspoken gift of knowing intimate details about others that I had no business knowing.

It wasn't until my first year in junior college that I had a conversation about auras. I was taking a cultural anthropology class where I met a man named André. He would become my study partner and ground zero of my spiritual awakening. André was taking a parapsychology class with a professor named Christelle and he always wanted to talk more about this class than study. He shared with me about telekinesis, telepathy, auras and other things he was learning. The more he talked the more fascinated I became.

Up until this point I'd never heard the word aura, yet the more he described them, the more it sounded like what I had been seeing my whole life. I shared my experience at church as a child and he was fascinated and wanted to know more. He questioned me incessantly. Hard as I tried to explain how to see them, the more frustrated he became that he couldn't. He told me that I was lucky and gifted. I thought that was strange. My whole life I assumed that everyone could see them. He insisted that I meet Christelle and later that week I did. During our meeting, André was clamoring to tell her about my ability to see auras. I was embarrassed. She encouraged me to enroll in her parapsychology class the next semester, and I did.

During this course I learned about many gifts I assume I was born with. But as I shared what I was learning in class with friends and family, it became apparent that it was not a topic people wanted to discuss or accept. So I rarely talked about or shared my ability to see auras unless it was obvious someone was open to it.

During a lecture, Christelle shared with us that she was telepathic. She explained that telepathy was the ability to pick up images or events off the energy signature imprinted on inanimate objects. To demonstrate she asked each of us to give her something we had worn or carried on a daily basis for the past several days or weeks. She turned down the lights then asked us to sit on the floor in a circle. She held up one item at a time and asked whom it belonged to. Once she identified the owner, she closed her eyes and slowly shared her impressions aloud. She made her way around the room to every student and with each reading was able to share something she would have no way of knowing. When she picked up my keychain and searched the faces in the room I raised my hand and she nodded. I thought my keychain would be perfect as it was something I carried with me every day. She closed her eyes, took a couple of deep breaths and said, "Oranges, I see lots and lots of oranges. Were you anywhere near oranges?" To my amazement, I told her it was just the day before my mother and sister had bought two 25-pound boxes of oranges and were making orange marmalade. I had been there, keychain in my pocket. She smiled. My mind was reeling. I wondered if she could smell oranges on the keys? I smelled nothing.

It was after this class that I told Christelle more about seeing auras, which led to another realization. My whole life, whenever I would get in close proximity to someone, I could hear tones. The closer I get, the louder they get and the pitch changes. She had never heard of this and couldn't explain it other than suggesting that I was picking up a person's life force. I realized the third gift was the ability to pick up on energy frequencies not only in light form, but also in sound.

On the weekend after this class, I went to a small party with a group of friends. Everyone was sharing stories about the classes they were taking and when it was my turn I told them about my parapsychology course. Everyone seemed interested. When I started explaining telepathy and shared the story about my professor picking up on the oranges from my keychain, eyes started rolling. One of the girls at the party and I kept talking about it after everyone else had moved on. She asked me if I would try telepathy on her. I really wanted to and I appreciated that she didn't think it was ridiculous. She announced to the six of us sitting in the living room that I was going to do a reading. Everyone quieted down and listened, some smirking. I asked her to get me an item that had significant meaning to her like a piece of jewelry or a photograph. She went to her bedroom and came back with a ring her grandmother had given to her when she was a young girl. As I held it in the palm of my hand, eyes closed, a movie began to play in my head. In slow motion I flew into the scene like a bird from the night sky looking down at a mobile home in the middle of a field. I flew through the front door, hovered in the air and watched the scene unfold in front of me.

There she was standing at the sink washing dishes. I shared with everyone what I was seeing: the back of her head and blond curly locks of hair hanging over her shoulders and down her back. From the left came an older woman walking toward her. As she came closer to the sink, I noticed that she held a knife in her hand and raised it in the air as if to stab her in the back. Sensing someone behind her, she turned around. A struggle ensued as she tried to protect herself. She cut her hand, but was able to confiscate the knife and subdue her attacker. When

I opened my eyes in confusion and shock at what I was seeing, she was crying. She looked at me shaking her head and said, "How did you know that?" The whole room was quiet. With tears in her eyes she explained that her mother was schizophrenic and one night while washing dishes, had tried to stab her. The mother was hospitalized shortly thereafter and on and off for many years. She went on to tell me that she lived in a mobile home at the time. My stomach was full of butterflies and my heart was racing with adrenaline. The images I saw were real.

I was terrified. How could I know this? How could I see this? Images from the movie *The Exorcist* flashed in my head. I went home and before I went to sleep, I removed the crucifix my grandmother had given me from my nightstand drawer and hung it above my bed. I prayed to God that the devil had not possessed me.

I had a bad nightmare that night. I was lying in bed, the crucifix hanging behind me on the wall and two figures covered head to toe in black robes were at my side chanting, "You are possessed, you are possessed." I tore off the hoods to reveal it was my mother and sister. I woke up in a cold sweat and said out loud, "God, I will never do that again, just don't let me be possessed!" Little was I to know that telepathy would be my fourth gift, and I would use it again only much later in life and for much different reasons.

Growing Up Different

Growing up in Los Angeles in the 60s as a sensitive, tuned-in boy presented a challenge for my mother and father. While other boys were playing little league baseball, I wanted to learn how to knit. I was skinny, anemic and enjoyed playing dress-up in my mother's high heels and mink stole. The family called me Prissy and I would put on a show to uproarious laughter. I was keenly tuned in to having crushes on my male teachers and friends. Even though there was nothing sexual about it at that age, it didn't stop me from realizing I was different. I grew up experiencing life from a perspective most boys didn't. I eventually learned that it was bad for boys to think and behave the way I did so I tried to hide it. If I behaved like the other boys, I was accepted, but if I didn't, I was rejected. This started a pattern of trying to be someone other than who I was. One of the many lessons I've had to learn in this life.

I had a very close relationship with my father. He and I bonded and genuinely liked many of the same things. There was a soul connection and I often felt like we had the same physical constitution and thoughts on just about everything. I was a carbon copy of him. I remember most of my childhood hanging out together, watching scary movies and listening to stories about his childhood in Italy. Each night when tucking me into bed he would tell the story of the continuing adventures of Joe the crocodile. By the time I was 11 years old I knew he and mom were going to get a divorce. I would think about it while lying in bed at night. I had a constant knot in my stomach. While I sensed it intuitively, there were outward signs as well, most notably the inability for him and my mom to get along. There was no humor, understanding or bending, only rigid offense to every small or big thing often resulting in fights. They clearly saw things very differently. Mom stopped having fun shortly after the children arrived and was resentful and unhappy. On the night he left, he and my mom were having a serious conversation in the kitchen. I hid in the dining room and listened to them talking about dad getting an apartment and when us children would visit. At this point I burst into the kitchen and asked, "Dad, are you moving out?" When mom looked at me with sad eyes my worst fears became a reality. I was unable to do anything other than run to my room, slam the door and yell, "You don't care about me!" While I lay crying in my room, I could hear dad's car start. But by the time I made it out the front door he was already backed out of the driveway and heading down the street. I ran after the car as fast as I could screaming hysterically "Dad, don't leave!" but it was too late, he was already gone. I fell to the street in a slump sobbing inconsolably. My mother came out after me, picked me up and brought me back in the house. She later told me she almost reconciled with him because it broke her heart to see me so sad. I cried for days. I lost my anchor and sense of safety that night. This emotional and powerful event would create behaviors in my life that taught me several lessons I came here to learn, overcoming co-dependency, fear of death and abandonment.

These issues plagued me for years and through many relationships. My dad's reason for being in my life was to teach me how to overcome these fears with unconditional love.

Junior High and High School

The one thing I remember most about having my dad at home was the feeling of being safe. No matter where I was, or what I needed, he was always there for me. After the divorce, my mother moved us to Northern California with her new husband and life was very different. I was no longer safe.

I was coming into puberty and so was everyone around me at school. I wanted to be accepted so I played along and pretended at great struggle to fit in. I thought I was doing well until in junior high school the bulling and name-calling started and I couldn't understand why anyone would say and do these things. I would study myself in the mirror and watch the way I walked, the tone in my voice, the way I sat, the way I looked at people, the way I moved my hands, crossed my legs, dressed. I tried desperately to be just like everyone else, but it wasn't working very well.

I was short, skinny and only weighted 92 pounds in 8th grade. Inevitably, the bully of the day would threaten to kick my butt then push me into the lockers, punch my arms or shove me down the hall. I never told my mom or stepfather because I didn't want them to know, or worse yet, risk further exposing what was so obvious to everyone else. I didn't want them to judge me either. When I started high school the name calling accelerated and the attacks grew more violent. In my freshman year of high school I was hung on a hook by my jock strap in the locker room while some boys walked by, spit on me and called me names. Later it resulted in an unprovoked punch in the face without warning, which gave me the first of two black eyes in high school. My parents, who were friends with the perpetrator's parents, created an embarrassing and forced apology that only served to further increase the bullying. At age 15, during a homecoming party my junior year the violence hit its peak. I was talking with a group of classmates when out of nowhere I was knocked off my feet with a kick to my ankles. I felt the kicking against my body as I hit the ground and slurs filled the air. I tried to get up, but was punched hard in the face. A group of students stepped in to break up the attack. Humiliated and terrified, I ran to my friend's car, jumped in the back seat and locked the doors. Shortly after, my friend knocked on the window and I let her in. She told me, "Don't worry, they're just jerks and they've left." I begged her to take me home, but she and the others we came with wanted to stay and party. I had no choice, but to wait in the back seat for over an hour until they all decided to leave. I realized later that I really didn't have any friends with me that night. My body was bruised and aching, I had a black eye and my swollen lip was bleeding all over my shirt. Not a single person consoled me. I was alone. As I sat there for that long hour, I thought about being gay. No matter how hard I tried to deny it or hide it, people knew anyway. I also knew that these bullies secretly loathed themselves and were hiding their own feelings about attraction to the same sex. I knew that they didn't hate me; they hated that part of themselves. Somehow beating me up would prove to them and others they didn't have those feelings. While I was far from ready to accept who I was that night, I had two choices, sit on a pity pot or rise from the experience stronger. I did the latter. I grew a thick skin and swore that I would never let anyone break my spirit. What they say about adversity is true. What doesn't kill you makes your stronger. The bullying? It served one purpose; it made me a compassionate man. It made me kinder to people. It guided me to accept people for who they are and love them unconditionally. It was a secret awakening. It was exactly as it needed to be. Sometimes the greatest lessons are in the biggest challenges we have to overcome.

Junior College

After graduation from high school I left the bullying and insecurity behind and went to junior college in Northern, California. It was in there that I studied Parapsychology with Christelle and began to explore my gifts. Although my first experience with telepathy scared me, I still wanted to know more. The more I asked Christelle to elaborate on energy, auras and telepathy, the clearer it became that she didn't have the answers I needed. She would shrug her shoulders, give me a look through squinted eyes and say, "I can't help you."

Once she suggested I visit a psychic who lived in a little town just north of town. Her name was Beverly. At this point I was desperately looking for someone who understood me. Of course, my greatest fear was that she would know I was gay; something I was not yet ready or willing to admit to anyone. I was worried that she would say it out loud and I would be cast back into the nightmare of junior and senior high school days. With high school behind me I was somehow able to hide my sexuality without suspicion. With some trepidation I went to see her. Beverly was in her 70s, I was 19, a closeted gay man in search of answers. I was hoping that during this meeting she could tell me everything I needed to know about my gifts and uncertain future. Instead she sat across the table from me, held my hand and said, "Gary, I can tell you are very open, extremely intuitive and sensitive. I can see music in your future." Music? I didn't even play an instrument. I asked her if she was sure it was music and not acting. She was quite sure. I already knew I was open, intuitive and sensitive but music? That baffled me.

It was destiny that several months after my visit with Beverly I met my friend Greg in a natural history class. Greg played guitar and upon asking, he patiently showed me how to strum the basic chords. Greg and I became best friends. We played guitar, sang and drank wine for hours. He was always kind and never judgmental. He brought me into his circle of family and friends. Greg had the skill of gathering unlikely people together and bringing out the best in them. He gave me one of the greatest gifts in my life, music. Not only would he teach me how to play, it would be the beginning of a nearly 25-year career in music. Beverly was right. There was music in my future.

As I began to develop my guitar playing skills, music became the only thing that mattered to me. It was my best friend and the only way I could express and relate to my world, much of it painful and wrought with fear of coming to terms with my sexuality. I suffered terribly from anxiety and playing music was like meditating to me. When I played guitar and sang, it was a healing salve to my soul. Sadness and longing poured out from a place deep inside protected under layers of thick skin and scars. I could express my pain through music yet hide behind the song. It was easy to tell people I wrote it about someone else. It wasn't until later, when I began recording my music, that I could hear and feel the pain I was going through when I wrote it. For the first time I could cry and connect to the pain. Writing music helped me get through the darkest times in my life. Without it I don't know how I would have survived. I wrote hundreds of songs.

Music was so imbedded in my karma that before I could play a single chord on the guitar I wrote a song by plucking at four random strings to make a melody.

If I had the chance to be
The person that I'd like to be
I'd take these words and write a book
And maybe then you'd give me a look

I can see now that the lyrics to this song were a prediction in a way. I would take these words and write a book, but only 33 years later after recording four CD's and performing in front of thousands of people. Another amazing synchronicity that gives me undeniable proof that there is so much more to this life than meets the eye.

I always wished I had kept in touch with Beverly and asked her what else she saw in my future but didn't tell me.

University Days

I had graduated from junior college and went to live with my dad in Los Angeles. I was working at my uncle's deli for the summer when I received a call from Greg. He said, "I'm going to Humboldt State University and you should come with me!" So the wind blew me up North to Arcata, California.

During university, I tried hard to figure out who I wanted to be and what I wanted to do. I had this incredible feeling that something wonderful was going to happen. Spirituality and the unknown intrigued me. I often thought that at any given time a big hole in the universe would open up and I would walk into the light and disappear.

17

On the other hand, I was plagued with coming to terms with my sexuality in an anti-gay world. I was living a lie with my friends and family, and like a ship being tossed on a stormy sea, I didn't have a clue which way I would go.

At that time in my life, I wanted to work for the Forest Service so I could be close to nature. Earning a degree in Recreation Administration would be a good choice if I wanted to pursue that field. I felt the need to be outdoors. Nature was my sanctuary. I needed to be away from people, traffic and noise. It was during my junior high and early high school years that I fell in love with Mother Nature. I lived on a 600-acre ranch of pristine pines and breathtaking beauty. I walked up the creek side every day a half a mile from the house, sat on a rock and sang Cat Stevens songs. I would imagine I was singing to a crowd of people, but instead of people, it was the birds that would land near me, fish that would swim in the pools of water at my feet and my dogs that were the audience. I felt electrically charged and connected to every living thing around me.

Humboldt State was a happy place for me. No longer a tormented schoolboy, I was now a young man out to make sense of the world. During my first year I studied Native American shamanism and learned about Carlos Castaneda. I took comparative religion classes and soaked up everything I could about how the world perceived God. Of course, I had no idea then I would later meet Carlos Castaneda in person and he would ask me to apprentice under him.

During my years at university, I began to feel more at peace. I was far away from the cowboy towns of Northern California and the mindset was more liberal. While it still wasn't safe to come out, I was more comfortable in my own skin and less worried about what people thought of me. I had yet to either have a steady girlfriend or dare to venture into my gay proclivity. Friends would inevitably ask, "You're such a nice guy, why don't you have a girlfriend?" Girls wondered why I wouldn't ask them out and, if I did, why I wouldn't commit to another date. My mom and dad did too. I refrained from sharing my gifts or talking about them the same way I refrained from having a loving relationship. I wasn't ready to open my heart or reveal my true self. I had no concept of how to love myself let alone somebody else. I just couldn't find the strength to come out of the closet. I think I was waiting for someone to tell me it was okay, but it wasn't in those days. The questions continued to plague me. Should I pretend to be straight and have a relationship with a woman? Should I hide what I feel inside, where my heart comes from, what my intuition tells me? I struggled with every relationship I had with a woman because I was lying and ultimately that lie would hurt them. I could never get close because of that. Equally, I was hurting myself. I tried desperately, but it just didn't work.

I went to a lot of bars and parties. I liked being around people, but I was inundated with energy and thoughts that made being around them hard. At times I thought I was crazy. I couldn't shut off the voices in my head. I picked up on the thoughts of people, the movies of their life, the pain in their hearts, their feelings towards everything. I tended to be quiet and more tuned into the energy around me. I spent little time talking and more time listening, feeling and watching everyone closely. I saw so many people pretending to be somebody they weren't, just like me. I was looking for people like me. Maybe even somebody who had the same sexual feelings that I did. While there were many, we were all too afraid to acknowledge it.

I struggled with my psychic abilities and often felt that knowing things about people was a curse. What good is it to know a mentally unstable mother nearly killed her daughter? That a woman's uncle sexually abused her or that a boy's brother abused animals because his father abused him. The cacophony of images and movies in my head was endless, I could not shut it off. I was frustrated knowing too much. It made life harder. There were friends who were enemies, enemies who were friends. Confusing information coming at me in a sea of emotions as someone would speak knowing it wasn't what they meant. People pretending to be someone they are not. Conflicting messages like, I look great, but I hate myself, I'm laughing, but I'm so sad, I love you, but I'm sleeping with someone else. I would think myself crazy if it wasn't for the fact that inevitably, though not always immediately, the movies and the voices were true. I had still yet to figure out how to live with people, how to trust people, how to navigate through the conflicting world of life on earth. I graduated from Humboldt State with new experiences and a little closer to understanding that all the unexplainable abilities I was born with were an amazing gift to see, feel and hear energy but mostly unveil the truth.

Hollywood

After graduating from Humboldt State, I moved home to my father's house in Los Angeles and worked at my uncle's Italian deli. The Deli was the hub for our family and it was there I knew I could always go. I grew up in that deli and worked most summer breaks and holidays during high school and college. It was more fun than work because I could be with my grandmother and uncle daily, two of my favorite people. During this time I decided I wanted to try my hand at acting and took an acting class from a gentleman named Robert. Robert made a name for himself on Broadway and in Hollywood writing a string of successful musicals, screenplays, television shows and books. He was a kind gentle soul and taught classes in the living room of his house in Beverly Hills. It was during one of these classes that I met Christine. I resonated with her immediately. Like me, she was spiritual and looking for a break in Hollywood amongst the impossibly competitive crowd. We were both looking for that someone who could further our career. In Hollywood it isn't how talented you are, it's who you know. Robert was that someone to know.

Christine had already taken several classes from him and he was smitten with her. He was writing a screenplay about a young woman traveling across the country with her best friend on a spiritual journey. He had hopes of casting the movie himself and putting Christine in the starring role.

Christine and I became good friends. She was kind, loving and a highly evolved spiritual being. Besides an aspiring actress, she was a master of the Tarot. She called me "the babe in the woods" and felt I needed to be protected. She offered to teach me how to read the Tarot and I felt that it would somehow put me more in touch with my gifts. She started by explaining the meaning of each card. The instructions were, every night before bed I was to take one, say a special meditation and during my sleep I would assimilate its energy and become intimate with its true meaning. Christine could see something in me that I couldn't. She believed I was destined to be someone great. She told me that I was the purest soul she had ever met.

Each night I did as instructed and meditated on a new card and each morning I would reflect on any new insights I had gained. When I got to the card "The Fool", my life changed forever. Ever since the night I telepathically witnessed the girl being attacked by her mother, I was a little fearful of anything that could be demonic or dark. So, in addition to the meditation, I would pray and surround myself with white light asking for protection. I asked each night for a confirmation that what I was doing was right.

Up to this point, I never got one, nor did I know how it would look if I did. That night, I had tumultuous dreams. Nothing made sense. I was running toward the light, but falling down, getting up and running again. The closer I got to the light the more deeply connected I felt. The dream was a collage of colors, feelings and connections, but nothing was concrete. I was half asleep and half awake laying on my right side when a male voice said loudly in my ear, "Gary, wake up, your confirmation is that it is 6:14 a.m." I opened my eyes and looked at the wall, rolled over on my left side and there on the bedside table was a digital clock that read, 6:14 a.m. Now the chances of this being coincidence are 1 in 1,440. Like the vision of my friend's mother trying to stab her, this was no coincidence, this was another nudge in my spiritual side saying, "Gary, go forward, do not be afraid, I AM here to protect you."

There was no devil trying to possess me, or demon trying to take my soul. It was simply a divine sign and a gift. It gave me strength to believe that we are all somehow connected and that there is something so much bigger than what is in front of our eyes. Something that ties us together in an unending string of lights, bouncing particles of energy streaming from one subconscious mind to another, a conduit that brings the messages and beholds the light of being. The very particles that say, we are here, we are everywhere and love is the answer. Don't lose your connection Gary, it's right here, don't lose it. Tears fell from my eyes, my human skin and hair standing on edge and love coursing through my veins in this instant of confirmation. Gary, it's 6:14 a.m., time to get started.

Shortly thereafter, Christine met a music producer and moved to England. Things just weren't the same. I took a few more acting classes with Robert, but I lost my desire to pursue the dream. I moved out of my father's house and into an apartment on Garfield Place in Hollywood and got a job with American Airlines. This time the journey would lead me to a woman named Brenda.

Brenda

Brenda had a crystal shop on Melrose in the storefront of a flower shop. She had several tables covered in fine colored sand and throughout had artfully placed the most amazing polished and natural crystals. She took pride in selling only the finest specimens available. There were giant Amethyst geodes and rutilated quartz, obelisks and towering formations of every kind. I was instantly drawn into her space and we immediately hit it off. Like Christine, Brenda was highly evolved spiritually. My energy was not at all odd to her and she encouraged me to use my gifts. Wherever we would go she would prod me with questions like, "What are you picking up?"

Brenda was 20 years my senior and in many ways became my mentor. She was able to help me see things in a new light, one of experience. I was 24 and trying to figure out my purpose in life. She was 44 and lonely. Her apartment was full of candles, crystals and heavenly scents. The energy was healing and I loved being there. I spent many nights in her spiritual cocoon. During one of our all night conversations I'll never forget her asking me, "What do you want to do with your life?" my response, "I just want to load and unload baggage on an airplane." We both laughed hysterically and she said, "That's a start!"

Brenda had a sadness about her, an inability to accept herself for who she was. Perhaps I resonated with her because I was the same. Together we soothed each other's loneliness and explored in cryptic code my reluctance to have a loving and sexual relationship. What I was unable to say was that I could not give my heart to a woman when I would later end up hurting her by not being true to my nature. Brenda lived in the heart of West Hollywood and was surrounded by gay men. Of course, she knew I was as well but never pried. She just offered me unconditional acceptance, little gems of spiritual knowledge and a lifetime of experience. She told me life was full of darkness and bad people were everywhere. She worried that I was a babe in the woods, a bright light and that someone would hurt me or take advantage of my naiveté. I thought I could take care of myself. I didn't think I was naïve and I wouldn't let anyone take advantage of me. But at 24, I did want to believe that everyone was good and nobody would ever intentionally hurt someone. If someone was hurtful, I was able to discern that it wasn't about me. I forgave easily.

I was beginning to view events in my life as karma with some lessons for me, some for others, all for some reason. I was evolving with Brenda. We were two souls perfectly placed in each other's life at the perfect time.

Brenda invited me to a party in Los Angeles and Carlos Castaneda was the guest of honor. I learned about him while taking a course on shamanism at Humboldt State. She felt strongly that I should go with her and that we should try to meet him. We were both excited.

A crowd of people gathered in the living room and Brenda and I stood in the back as Carlos gave a talk on alternate realities. When he was finished, he asked the audience if they had any questions. Hands kept going up around the room and after he would answer each one he would pause and look around the room for another hand. One of these times his eyes locked on mine for more than an intense few seconds. I stared back, but had to look away. I said to Brenda, "Did you see that?" She replied, "He was looking right at you." It was strange. I felt grabbed and then pulled by a very powerful force. The energy in the room was intense and vibrating frantically. When he was done answering questions, he walked right past several people waiting to talk to him and made a beeline directly to the back of the room and introduced himself to us. Brenda gushed, saying what an honor it was and without skipping a beat launched into telling him about me, and my telepathic abilities. I was beet red and embarrassed. I didn't know him other than I knew he was someone famous and didn't have a clue how he would react. I imagined he might think I was crazy. But I should have known that he would be the last person in the world to think that. Instead, he was very intrigued and listened intently, especially about the story of my friend who was nearly stabbed by her mother. He asked me to tell him the color of his aura, which I could see was intensely green. It was telepathy that peaked his interest the most. He looked deep into my eyes, cocked his head a little, squinted his eyes, then reached into his pocket and pulled out his wallet. He gave it to me and said, "Tell me what you pick up when you hold this." I looked at Brenda, then Carlos and with heart pounding in my chest I closed my eyes and held the wallet tightly in my hand. Suddenly I became him, I could feel what it was like to be inside of his body and I began to feel sick. I spoke out loud and told him this. I sensed a poison-like energy coursing through my veins and pain in my kidneys, stomach and heart. When I opened my eyes, he was wide-eyed and listening intently. Fans wanting to talk with him waited patiently around us and he could feel their pull. He took back his wallet, opened it and took out a business card, grabbed a pen from his shirt and proceeded to write down the name and number of his assistant, "Give her a call, I would like to meet with you alone so we can talk further." Then he turned directly to Brenda, stared her in the eyes and said, "You better not steal his energy 'bruja'!" flashed a smile, then turned to talk with someone else. Neither she nor I could wrap our heads around what just happened. We talked about it all the way home and Brenda laughed, "He called me a 'bruja'." I didn't even know what a "bruja" was until she told me it meant witch in Spanish. As I dropped her off, she exited the car turned around and asked me with a sly smile, "Are you going to call his assistant?" I said, "Sure, why not." A couple of days later I reached out to her and she told me he had been waiting for my call. She explained Carlos was doing an apprentice program with a select few people. I listened intently and had no idea what she meant by apprentice. She started quoting how much the program would cost and I immediately told her I couldn't afford it, "Oh no, Carlos wants you to join at no charge." She said it was a several week program and I would need to devote myself full-time. When I hung up I called Brenda. We were both excited and curious about what this program entailed and why he was offering it to me for free.

Later that night as I was lying in bed, I noticed the energy start to intensify and I could feel adrenaline start to rush through my body. The space in the room started swirling with sparks of light. I could always see energy but I had never seen it like this. I was dizzy, lightheaded and at times felt I was going to pass out, I was terrified. I felt plastered to the bed barely able to move. I reached for my bedside table, pulled the phone onto the bed and called Brenda. All I could say was, "Oh my God, Brenda, I think I'm going to die." She responded calmly, "Gary, take some deep breaths and relax." I told her I was sensing a very dark energy in the room and I was scared to death. It felt like someone was trying to suck the life out of me. I kept saying that I needed to go to the Emergency Room. My heart was pounding in my chest, my mouth was dry and I felt weak and poisoned. She reminded me over and over, "Call on the light Gary, surround yourself with light, close your eyes and surround yourself with light, nothing can hurt you, you are safe." I visualized the light surrounding me, yet when I opened my eyes all I could see were sparks flying around the room. As I looked around at the light display, I noticed that sitting on top of my highboy dresser was the outline of a small body the size of a boy with a wooden Mexican folk art devil mask on. I knew instantly it was Carlos. I spoke his name out loud to Brenda. She began to calmly assure me, "You are stronger than him Gary, send light, send him light, tell him he cannot touch you because you are light. He cannot have you." This went on for about 20 minutes. Brenda guided and empowered me to find the light inside myself and project it outward toward Carlos. I repeated with her over and over, "You cannot have my light, I AM of the light and you are of the dark. I release you." It started loud and frantic and after several minutes we were almost whispering. When I opened my eyes the frenetic energy and Carlos were gone. The room was pitch black. No longer were sparks flying and a calm was within the room and me. I never heard from Carlos Castaneda or his assistant again.

Once again I learned that my gifts were not to be used for entertainment or put on public display. It would only attract dark influences or people who might wish to use me as an instrument for their personal gain. I AM certain that Carlos intended to use my gifts for the wrong reasons. The battle we fought was a test and it was clear to me why he never called me again. He came into my life to teach me a valuable lesson about the power of darkness and light. Another miraculous experience that further solidified my belief in the unseen world. As Carlos would say, an alternate reality that is clear to some and impossible to many. I emerged that night stronger and surer of my direction and beliefs. I often think about where my life would have taken me if I had chosen to go in a different direction that night. Carlos expired 11 years later from liver cancer.

Hollywood was a pipe dream. There were so many beautiful and talented people and so few parts. My headshot got me a few auditions, but you had to have that something that made you stand out from everyone else. It was time to move on. A dream brought me to Hollywood and the outcome wasn't fame, it was enlightenment. The real reason I came was to meet Christine and Brenda. The dream confirmation and spiritual battle with Carlos changed my life forever. Both experiences were healing for me. I suffered with anxiety and fear of dying for most of my life and now I could see there was no real death. We simply transcend our bodies and enter into the realm of energy where Carlos traveled and waged wars and where dreams transmitted messages from beyond. It was in the energy, I just knew it. I packed up my things, said goodbye to Brenda and moved to San Diego to begin the next chapter in my life.

Near Death on the Fire Line

In San Diego I found a job as a firefighter with the U.S. Forest Service. It was work I could always fall back on since I had several seasons of experience working summer breaks from college. We called ourselves adrenaline junkies. It was one day while on a fire that I had a near death experience that reopened the portal to the world of particles and energy. I was on an assignment in Yosemite fighting a massive fire. The team and I were patrolling an area of extinguished fire looking for hot embers that could possibly ignite the fire again or blow in the wind and start a fire in another area. We were at the top of a steep mountain where a fire line had been cut by a bulldozer straight across the top of the peak. The fire had burned up one side in the underbrush without igniting the pine trees in its path then crossed over and burned in the underbrush down the other side. Strong winds started to blow and it quickly rekindled the fire and pushed it up into the crowns of the trees. As the trees burst into flames, the fire began to burn back up the hill this time creating an inferno 100-feet high. The fire was coming up the hill at rapid speeds fueled by high winds right to where we were standing. Blowing embers ignited the crowns of the trees on the other side of the cleared fire line so now we were sandwiched between two massive walls of flames while standing on a small 10-foot wide path. The heat was so intense that the captain told us to ready our fire shelters. We learned in fire training that in the event you were surrounded by fire, these portable shelters would be your only chance of survival. They were slightly larger than a 6-foot tall man and were foil-like, fire retardant, heat deflecting shields in the shape of a small tent. The idea was to grab a strap with the tip of both boots and then both hands, drop to the ground on your stomach and a little tent structure would pop up around your body protecting you for a limited time from the heat and smoke. We had them ready to go, off our belts and out of their bags. The smoke was thick and I couldn't see much around me. A dampened bandana covered my mouth and nose and helped to reduce the amount of smoke I was inhaling. I listened intently to hear the captain's commands. At one point, I was overcome by anxiety and started to panic. My lips became numb and my heart began to race. The smoke made me dizzy, short of breath and I hyperventilated. I thought I was going to die and started preparing myself. I imagined the entire scenario. I would hopefully pass out from the smoke first but if not, I would feel the heat against my skin, a moment of terrible pain then pass out. Fire would consume me and then I would leave my human body and become energy. I remembered my experience with Carlos Castaneda and the frenetic molecules dancing around the room. I could see particles of light vibrating everywhere. I heard someone on my team yell out, "Should we deploy?" The captain replied, "Hold". I could hear him radio the engine to see if the fire was burning over the fire line ahead of us. Everything seemed to move in slow motion. I closed my eyes, slowed my breathing and a sense of peace came over me. I began to vibrate in sync with the energy around me. A voice said, "Not much longer Gary, just step into the light." There was no sadness, no fear or regret, only surrender. I was in a state of euphoria and completely letting go. I felt myself drifting away when I was jolted to attention by the voice of the captain yelling, "Run!" I opened my eyes and saw my team take off down the fire line after him. I felt the heat burning my face and smoke filling my lungs as I quickly followed after them. We ran for what seemed like an eternity then one by one emerged from the smoke and flames into a large open area where several fire engines were parked. In a few moments time I went from paralyzing fear, near death and complete surrender to complete safety. Everyone was breathing a sigh of relief and heads were shaking, "That was close." After this experience, I was more confident that death didn't mean the end. Maybe it was the vibrating energy or the voice saying, "Just step into the light." Either way, my beliefs became stronger that day and my life took on new meaning. Some might say I was only hyperventilating but I know better. It was something telling me again that everything is not what it seems, "Don't be afraid Gary, I AM everywhere and you are one with me."

Kim

The next fire season I met Kim. Like so many other teachers in my life, she instantly took me into her heart and home. At the time I was in less than optimal living arrangements. After sharing this with her she insisted that I move out and found me a place to rent right next to her house. This would be the first time I ever lived entirely on my own. I always lived with roommates up to that point in my life and with them there wasn't ever the option to come out, at least without the possibility of having to find a new place to live. Kim was an exercise and fitness nut that worked out incessantly. She inspired me to be in shape, eat right and take care of myself. She quickly became my confidant and then ever so slowly and gently was able to help me see that being gay was normal. She would often assure me there was nothing wrong with me; I was normal and worthy of all the love and acceptance that any straight person had. She was strong, kind and protective. I was able to share with her my feelings for a fellow fire fighter. I told her I cared for him deeply and that he was the only man I would ever consider being "that way" with. She told me compassionately, "Gary, I want you to think about this. If you have the capacity to feel this way about him, wouldn't it be possible to feel this way about another man?" I didn't answer right away, but the thought stuck with me for many days before deciding that she was right. Not only was she right, I could no longer pretend that I wasn't gay.

One night Kim decided to take me out to a women's bar called The Flame. She figured it would be a non-threatening introduction to the gay scene and it would be my first experience in a gay bar. It was safe and not overwhelming. She took me there a couple of times a week to play pool and dance. Every now and then other men would show up and it gave me a chance to see I wasn't alone. While this was comforting, I was still scared to death. To act on my sexual desires would mean I might expose myself to HIV and AIDS. I came out in a world of men dying all around me. It seemed every news report and article in the papers was talking about this devastating disease plaguing the gay community. Even though the earlier stigma and frantic fear around AIDS being transmitted by hugging or kissing was over, it was still looming. I was witness to many innocent people succumbing to a painful demise. There was a dark cloud over the gay community. The papers were full of obituaries and the coffee house I frequented had a memory wall that grew with names daily.

I decided that I wanted to help in some way and so I volunteered at Special Delivery, a food delivery service run by a woman named Ruth out of her restaurant in Mission Hills. Ruth and her crew prepared meals for people with HIV and AIDS who were home bound and in desperate need of good nutrition. My job was intake coordinator. I visited prospective clients, interviewed them and determined if they met the criteria to receive meals.

On my first visit to a client, I stood outside the door knocking for several minutes to no avail. Just as I was ready to give up, I heard a faint voice call out from inside, "Just come in." I opened the door and climbed a flight of stairs and there I found a man sitting in a chair who looked to be somewhere in his 80s. He was skeletal and yet his stomach distended to proportions of a woman nine months pregnant, his face covered in blisters and arms in dark colored lesions. I introduced myself, sat down, looked at the questionnaire and set it aside. He asked me what information I needed from him and I explained the interview was only a formality and I didn't need anything. I told him that meal delivery would start right away. He seemed relieved and grateful. We spent about 30 minutes sharing stories and then I had to go on to the next client interview. Before I left I asked if there was anything I could do for him and he shook his head no and said, "Thank you for the visit." I gave him a hug goodbye, went downstairs, got in my car and sobbed uncontrollably. This man was 42-years-old.

Eventually, Kim took me to a men's bar so I could see how the "other half" lived. My first night out was to a small club called Peacock Alley. I was a little nervous and didn't know what to expect. Kim repeated the words that seemed to follow me everywhere, "You're such a babe in the woods". When I walked through the door everything unfolded in slow motion. Men were everywhere, sitting at the bar, at tables, playing pool, dancing and several checking me out as I walked across the room. I was overwhelmed and found myself crouching behind Kim uncomfortably like her shadow. Kim ordered us beers while looking around the room and poking me in the side, "What do you think of him?" followed by my standard reply, "He's okay." Eventually she left me alone to use the restroom. When she returned, she grabbed my arm and walked me to a smaller room with another bar in it. She told me she wanted me to meet someone. When we got to the bar, three shots of cinnamon schnapps were lined up and she handed one to me, the other to a stranger and kept the last one for herself. A quick cheers and down the hatch they went. With my throat still burning, she introduced me to a man whom she claimed was a friend of hers. He and I ended up talking for a couple of hours that night. This led to several dates and eventually developed into a five-year relationship. He was my very first relationship and my first love. Kim later told me that she had met him on her way to the restroom. This one haphazard meeting created a relationship that would teach me more about myself than any other ever has.

Having never been in a committed relationship before, I moved full speed ahead with reckless abandon. I was finally living the dream I had my whole life, to fall in love and spend the rest of my days with someone. I lived in a state of hypnotic happiness for the first three years until a series of events morphed the last two into a slow and painful unraveling. It was during these last two years that I met my best friend and twin soul Lorraine. She would be my teacher and guide for next the several years of my life.

Lorraine

Lorraine and I met while working as customer service representatives at a printing company. We too had an instant connection. We spent every lunch talking about God, spiritual evolution and karma. We were so connected that we barely needed words to communicate. It was clear that we were family and had shared many lifetimes together. Our reconnection in this life was a great source of happiness and joy for both of us. At work I didn't come out to her and it wasn't until we made plans to have dinner one night that I told her about my partner. The first words out of her mouth were, "Thank God! Now we can be friends." We both laughed. In fact, we laughed hysterically for many years. We had the ability to simply crack each other up. Wherever we went, there was uproarious laughter. It was a gift. Since I had not been able to share my spiritual journey for a long time, I was excited and Lorraine was not only interested, she was eager to listen and share. I shared everything about my life at lightening speed. She would say, "Slow down, we have plenty of time." "If you tell me too much now, we won't have anything to talk about later." Of course always with a big smile and her sweet giggle. Lorraine, her mother, stepfather and several family members were devotees of the Self Realization Fellowship founded by Paramahansa Yogananda. I recognized the name immediately. She asked me if I had ever read *Autobiography of a Yogi* and then it hit me. Christine asked me the very same question years before. In fact, she gave me a copy and told me I had to read it. It sat on my bookshelf with an earmark on page 10 since then. It seemed that every time I picked it up to read I would get to page 10 and that was as far as I could go. We may own a book for several years, but until the time is right, it will gather dust. Upon Lorraine's insistence, I picked it up again and began to read. This time the pages turned and I could not put it down. I soaked up every word of its wisdom and enlightenment. I fell asleep each night reading it and had the most magical dreams with Yogananda in them. In one such dream, Yogananda came to me and led me to his secret hiding place when he was a boy. He showed me several books that his gurus had given him and photos he was hiding in a wooden box. As I was looking through everything, he turned to me, our eyes locked and he said, "Gary, I love you." eyes beaming with light. I began attending Self-Realization Fellowship each Sunday. The sermons given by Brother Mitrananda had me riveted to my seat. I developed the guru disciple relationship with Yogananda and all the saints of SRF. For the first time in my life, I began to meditate with purpose and started the Self- Realization Fellowship Lessons. I began to understand more about energy, why I had gifts and how my soul had evolved over many lifetimes. Things started to make sense. There were always unexplained lessons in my life and now I understood that no matter how painful they were, there was a valuable lesson in them. Sometimes it took years to understand, other times months and occasionally it was instant. On March 7th while meditating at the SRF Meditation Gardens in Encinitas, I asked for confirmation and Yogananda came to me. Sparkling light moved across the gardens and enveloped me with divine love. His presence was everywhere and came in waves of light vibrating through me and bringing a smile to my face. I thanked him out loud and heard his reply, "This is a special day." My first thought was, of course it is, I have my confirmation, you came to see me. After returning home I read that on March 7th Yogananda left his body. Yet another gift that confirmed I was on the right path. Frequently synchronicities such as this would come and serve to solidify that my spiritual beliefs were truth.

One of the greatest fears I have had to overcome in this life is the fear of dying. It started in my youth and flourished well into adulthood. It would manifest itself incessantly with a palpitating heart, dry mouth and adrenaline coursing through my body. Paralyzing anxiety took me to the Emergency Room many times with doctors and nurses rushing in to examine the seemingly healthy young man with the palpitating heart. It was the same thing each time, straps on my chest, electrocardiograms to rule out dangerous heart conditions, blood work and the same diagnosis every time, "You're having an anxiety attack. Have you ever thought of seeking counseling for this?"

I was always left reassured, yet embarrassed. I couldn't see that these attacks were just my inability to deal with life and the unacceptable circumstances I was in. I was in a relationship with a man who if my intuition was correct, was not right for me. My intuition had never steered me wrong before, yet I chose to live in denial rather than face the loss of a dream. It was too painful. I shared my suspicions with Lorraine and only she knew about my trips to the Emergency Room. Each time it was the same gentle line of questioning, "Gary, why do you think you are having anxiety?" She gently prodded, "Do you trust your intuition?" Our heads nodding up and down, "Then, what is it about you that that makes it okay to stay in this relationship? This isn't about him, this is about you." The message in her calm and loving way rang clear, "Gary, when the pain gets great enough, you will choose yourself." Lorraine taught me some powerful lessons about love and letting go. She taught me that it was okay to put myself first and if I did, no matter what, I would be okay. And no matter how hard the pain was right now, once I got to the other side I would know equal or greater happiness. She would repeat, "Gary, I promise you. Do you trust me? Let go." When I finally did let go and allow myself to experience the heart shattering break-up, I realized that I would not die, I would survive, I would be stronger and happier than I ever imagined and I would learn that all my intuitions were true.

Lorraine was in recovery from alcoholism for many years and had over a decade of sobriety. She was in a Twelve

Step Program, had a sponsor and worked on herself every day. To me she was an amazing human being if not an angel of love and light. I never once heard her say a disparaging word about anyone. She understood forgiveness and unconditional love. I once told her that I looked forward to growing old with her and was saddened by her reply, "Gary, I'm going to die young. I'm leaving here in my early 50s. I have work to do on the other side. This is something I've known my whole life." I was devastated at the thought of losing her. "Why?" I asked. She would only say, "I don't need to be here any longer." I didn't want to believe it.

As the years went by, I had a couple more relationships that were less painful and of shorter duration. Boundaries became easy to set. Putting myself first and trusting my intuition became priorities. Lorraine suggested that before I started looking for another relationship I should make a list of all the things I wanted and then not settle for anything less. I took her advice and made the following list; must not be afraid of spirituality, must have been in a long-term relationship, must have a good relationship with parents, must have a good job, must have a car, must be kind to waiters, must not have sex for six dates. I met my soul mate Steve on March 31st, 1995. Lorraine accepted him into the family with open arms and her intuition confirmed mine. He was a good man. We spent time as a family attending Self Realization Fellowship, holidays and weekly dinners together. Her entire family accepted my partner and I as one of their own.

Lorraine called me upset one day to tell me that her stepfather Christopher was diagnosed with cancer that had metastasized throughout his body and there wasn't long for him to live. We were all devastated, but having been a devotee of Self-Realization Fellowship (SRF) for many years, he was not afraid to die. He continued to meditate for hours each day and stay positive even through the most painful periods of the disease. Lorraine's mother Sarah was at his side the entire time. The two of them had an inspirational love that was seen and felt by everyone around them. At the end of his life, during one of my visits to the hospital, two Brothers from SRF came to pay their respects. Christopher told them with a smile that he was ready to go and was waiting for Yogananda to come. It was a couple of days later with Lorraine and Sarah at his side that he opened his eyes wide, sat up in bed and said, "Oh God, Oh Master, I didn't know, I didn't know. Oh Jesus, I didn't know." He looked at Lorraine and then Sarah and said, "I have to go now. I love you all." He took his last breath and left his body. It was about a week later Christopher came to me in a dream. He and I were in an embrace. I felt the embrace getting uncomfortable and he held me closer, looked me right in the eyes and said, "It's only love Gary, nothing more. Only love." And so it is only love that matters as we reunite with Source.

Over the years the family, my partner and I watched Lorraine's kids grow up and then, we painfully witnessed the slow unraveling of her life. It began with an accident. While attending a party, she fell down a steep driveway and sustained a compound fracture to her lower leg that sent her to into emergency surgery to repair the bone and severed nerves on top of her foot that the bone punctured. Her suffering was unbearable. Medication relieved the pain until addiction came and took over her life once again. I tried in vain to help her as the increasing doses took over and pushed her further away. I tried everything I could think of. I reached out to her friends in recovery and her sponsor all of whom she had pushed away. With each attempt she would insist, "You don't understand what it's like. You are judging me." My heart ached. No matter how hard I tried, the Lorraine I knew was slipping away. The last time I saw her for many years she was lying down in bed asleep with a lit cigarette in her mouth burned to the filter. When I woke her she looked at me with half open eyes and smiled ear to ear, "Gary! It's good to see you." Her smile revealed her teeth were rotted away from narcotic lollypops. She was heavily medicated and struggled to make sentences through her slurred speech. I pleaded with her, "Lorraine, please let me get you some help." I reminded her of the Program and her friends in recovery. She told me that her husband was taking care of her now and she would be fine. She scolded me for judging her. I couldn't bear seeing her this way. When I left I called her sponsor one last time and was reminded that there was nothing I could do; it was up to her. I remembered the serenity prayer that Lorraine taught me. "God, grant me the serenity to accept the things I cannot change, the courage to change the things I can and the wisdom to know the difference."

She moved to Colorado to be close to her sons and I lost contact.

Several years later, on a cruise ship in the middle of the Baltic Sea near Russia, my mobile phone rang. It was Lorraine. She asked if she could come out to San Diego and stay with me. She wanted to clear her head. I could tell by her slurred words that she was still using. I told her yes and I would call her upon my return. I had her number saved in my mobile phone. I believe now that this was my last chance to help her. When I returned home, her phone number no longer worked nor did the last email I had for her. I tried in vain for years to find her online to no avail.

In 2011 while visiting a new chiropractor, I ran into Lorraine's daughter Paula. It was by no chance that she was working as a massage therapist at this office. It was a sweet reunion and we vowed to spend time together. Paula shared that she was sad and estranged from her mom and feeling the hopelessness of watching her fade away the same way I had years before. She said Lorraine's living conditions were bad and she had to distance herself from it.

Not long after our reconnecting, Paula called me with news that her grandmother, Lorraine's mother, was diagnosed with the very same cancer that her stepfather died from and was in her last days. She gave me the address where she was living and I went to visit. Sarah was receiving hospice care and her son and two daughters were staying with her helping around the clock. Arrangements had been made for the entire family to visit in the coming days, but on this day, it was our time to say goodbye. Her son had just finished caring for her and left us alone in the room. Sarah grabbed my hand and squeezed it, looked me in the eyes and said, "I love you Gary, you're like my own and you have to do something for me. Lorraine needs you. You have to help her, only you can do it, I mean it." I explained how I had tried in the past to no avail, but she repeated, "I don't care, you have to help her." It was a mother's final cry to save her baby while she herself was leaving. She knew Lorraine was not long for the world and was hoping that I could somehow stop it.

A couple of days later, Lorraine arrived. It had been many years since I'd seen her. We held each other close in an embrace and whispered, "I love you." It was emotional for both of us. I was saddened to see that she was still heavily medicated, smoking and now using marijuana. All of her front teeth were missing. She knew she needed help and told me for the first time in years that she was going to get it saying, "I have to." I gave her a big hug. This was the last time I saw her. I received a call from Paula in May of 2012 telling me her mother had slipped into a coma. She died shortly thereafter.

Lorraine knew that she would leave this world young. For the short time she was in my life, she held my hand and loved me unconditionally. She taught me valuable lessons about acceptance, letting go and mostly, unconditional love. While I know she is now part of the light that guides me, every time I think of her my heart aches.

One rarity that Lorraine and I experienced was remembering a past life we shared together in ancient Rome as brother and sister. Separated from her as a young boy when our parents were killed, I was sold into slavery to a wealthy family capable of unspeakable cruelty. I was a servant in the house and often used and tortured sexually. Lorraine was the oldest child and raised our siblings the best she could. When I could I would sneak out of the house to meet up with her and share stories of my miserable existence. She would encourage me to stay level-headed and when the time was right, run away. The day I mustered the courage and left, I ran as fast as I could to the spot that we had planned to meet. It was on the outskirts of the city in an open field with scattered trees. We took cover in the shade of one. It was hot and the sun was shining brightly. The fields were gold with tall grass and I lay crying in her arms. I knew this was the only way. If I returned I would be subjected to unspeakable horror and if I ran they would surely find and kill me. She held out a vial and said, "You don't have to suffer anymore my brother. It will be quick, I promise." I had no choice. I drank the liquid and immediately felt the tingling spread throughout my body. My breathing became labored and slowly, but painlessly I left my body. I looked down at myself in her arms jerking in time with the last beats of my heart. She held me close and sobbed. I whispered in her ear, "Thank you, I will see you again."

She couldn't see or hear me. This life it was she that took the poison. Once again I say, "Thank you, I will see you again."

Current

For me, Source is defined as the pure light particles that permeate the infinite universe and constitute the makeup of living unconditional love. When I speak of Source I AM talking about that divine place where only this energy exists and nothing more. It's a place found through conscious contact with God through meditation. It is a state of pure joy that often comes with tears that fall freely from my eyes. I know I AM with Source when the love I feel has no restrictions. It flows like an unobstructed river of light and aligns my soul in perfect vibration with it. I know Source because my DNA was activated. When I speak of activation, I AM referring to the DNA that makes up our human existence. In it there is a gene with the ability to activate our brains in a way that allows our human senses to experience what is happening in the spiritual realm. The spiritual realm is a place that most cannot see; a portal to divine wisdom that flows freely in the particles of energy that are everywhere. I was born with eyes that see, a body that feels and ears that hear energy. For some reason I was born awake, yet I believe that everyone has the ability to activate his or her DNA. It is our divine birthright. The reason why the gifts lay dormant is because we don't take the time to develop them through meditation. In order for activation to occur we must detach from our senses and from this worldly existence. The distractions that cloud our thinking are endless. Until we get into the habit of slowing down, being in the moment and removing ourselves from the pervasive thoughts and senses, we won't find conscious contact with God or activate the gene that opens the portal. While the portal will open and close, being mindful of our senses can control when and where. Mindfulness comes with careful practice of meditation, letting go of our attachments, egos and the expectations of who we think we should be. The door opens when we are true to our nature, honest and forgiving of ourselves and generous to others. One only needs to be still and observe the energy at work.

Oprah

On July 21, 2014 my niece sent me an email that would change my life forever. It was an invitation to a weekend retreat with Oprah Winfrey called, "The Life You Want". She wrote, "I don't know why, but I really feel this will change my life and I need something right now. I'm determined to go. Do you want to join me?" I told her I would think about it and let her know.

Without thinking, I started researching online and found two tickets on Stub Hub. In less than 15 minutes, I had purchased tickets, booked a hotel and flights. I sent her an email, "I have the tickets in hand and we are going!" She replied, "I'm crying! Pure Joy! I haven't been this excited about something in a long time and I wouldn't want to share this life-changing experience with anyone but you!" I really wanted this for my niece. She had been struggling to find herself and working tirelessly at three jobs. This was the first time she had shown openness to exploring her spiritual side. I had sent her Sufian Chaudhary's book *World of Arch Angels* and a couple of books by Wayne Dyer but she was not ready to read them. I hoped for her to get a taste of elevated consciousness and being open to seeing Oprah and Deepak Chopra was an excellent start. I had recently finished reading Wayne Dyer's *Wishes Fulfilled* and Godfrey Ray King's *I AM Discourses* and on some level felt that this might be good for me as well. What I didn't realize at the time was that I wasn't doing this for my niece; she was doing it for me.

The weekend was an amazing experience filled with wisdom, unconditional love and an incredible amount of positive energy. All the speakers had an important message, but the most powerful one for me was from a meditation led by Oprah called "Creating The Life You Want." This single experience would change me forever. At the end of this meditation, she told us to sit in silence and wait for what she called "the whispers" and they would tell us everything we need to know. She was right. Every day during meditation they come as a soft voice vibrating into my consciousness with their profound insights. I have used her meditation every day since that weekend. It is to this discipline that I credit the full activation of my spiritual self. I AM no longer the same person I was and I AM truly living the life I want.

Destiny has a way of taking us exactly where we need to go and so a whisper came one day that told me, "Gary, write a book so that others might awaken to the truth." I had never written anything other than papers for school but I listened, trusted and started writing.

On the following pages are "the whispers" that came to me during several months of meditations. Each whisper is bolded and surrounded by quotation marks. As I sat down to write about each one, I could see clearly that the wisdom I was receiving could be shared through the stories of my life. These whispers were once for me and now they are for you. Each whisper is meant to stand-alone but is often interwoven with the others.

The Whispers

"With every thought you are manifesting your life."

During the Oprah weekend, I learned about manifesting the life I want by visualizing it in fine detail every day during meditation. It also helped me retrace the steps of my life to see that I had been visualizing and manifesting since I was born. I learned that the power of thought is the most important tool in creation. What I imagine or dream about over and over sets the creation wheel in motion and starts drawing to me what I AM putting out. Many call it the law of attraction. During my daily meditations I focus intently on creating the life of my dreams. My soul feels most at home when I AM in Hawaii and I feel strongly that this is where I want to live my life. So in my meditation, I imagine in detail that I AM living in Maui, building the house of my dreams and surrounding myself with people I want with me. Like a movie playing in my mind, I imagine myself flying from San Diego to Maui, landing, walking with my luggage through the airport to the rental car pick up, getting a car and driving to my house. I arrive at the gated entrance, press the remote, the gate opens and I proceed down the long driveway. The house is directly on oceanfront property. I park the car and enter through the front door. When I get inside I can see the house just as I designed it with concrete floors and vaulted wood beamed ceilings. Here love, good friends and family surround me. I shift my thoughts to God and Divine Love tuning into Source. I eventually arrive at a place in my meditation where I break apart into particles and become light. I feel my soul become one with everything in the universe. I AM pure unconditional love. My light is one with the planets, stars and infinity. I AM one with Source. I AM God, the most powerful creator in the universe. I wait in silence for the whispers to come.

It was only six weeks after starting Oprah's meditation, I found myself on a plane heading for Maui. I was astonished to see my daily mediation come to life in real time. The flight across the Pacific was perfect and exactly as I imagined each day in meditation. We landed, walked through the airport and took a shuttle to the rental car lot, picked out a car, loaded up and started driving to our rental house. I had researched online the week before and found a house to rent outside of Paia overlooking the ocean. As we followed the directions on the GPS, I smiled as it told us to turn left onto Door of Faith road. Immediately everything started looking familiar to me. We drove up to the very gate I visualized, punched in the code and drove down a tiny dirt road to the house. When we stepped inside the front door, I could see the wood beamed ceilings. This was the house I had created in silence for weeks. For five days I was in bliss and spent hours meditating. It was there I started writing this book. It was there I began to truly believe in the law of attraction.

Right before leaving San Diego, I downloaded the book *World of Arch Angels* by Sufian Chaudhary. I started reading it on the plane over and I found it instantly inspired and powerful. Sufian talked about his journey to enlightenment after meeting Archangel Uriel. I related to him on many levels and knew he was channeling something profound. I began to visualize him as someone I wanted in my life as a teacher, a guide and a friend.

After five days of writing at the ocean house, we packed our bags and headed to the other side of the island to the Sheraton Kaanapali. One of my goals for this leg of the trip was to finish Sufian's book. I discovered *World of Arch Angels* after a co-worker and I were discussing Arch Angel Michael. We both felt a strong connection to him and she told me about a book she had just finished that I should read. She couldn't remember the name of it, but said if I searched "Amazon Kindle Arch Angel Michael" I would find it. The first thing that came up was Sufian's book. I assumed this was it so I downloaded it. While reading his book I felt not only a kinship, but also my understanding of the spiritual realm began to accelerate at light speed. At first the book read like science fiction, but slowly I began to realize that he was channeling energy from a very evolved source of ancient knowledge. As his book started referencing the *I AM Discourses* several times, everything he was saying began to resonate as truth to me. It seemed obvious that he had a master level understanding of the laws of this existence and came from a place that only few know, perhaps an unlimited understanding of the masterwork that is our Universe.

On our first night in Kaanapali, I stayed up late and finished Sufian's book. I was truly astonished by the revelations presented. As I often do, I said a prayer and asked for a confirmation of truth. I rolled over on my side and fell quickly into a deep sleep and started dreaming. I rarely ever remember my dreams, but in this one I had written a book. I was preparing to give a talk at a beautiful hotel somewhere in Hawaii. The entire event was set up in a garden room with beautiful flowers and plants everywhere. Tables were set for a meal and a podium surrounded by flowers was ready for me. I was nervous about speaking and was hanging out in the catering kitchen making last minute adjustments to my notes and talking with various "dream" people that included my partner and a co-worker. The event had started and it was time for me to speak. I was introduced and stepped up to the podium. I had all my notes and excerpts from my book ready to go, but as I started the introduction I looked down and realized that I couldn't read my notes. I squinted and struggled, but I just couldn't make out the words. I was embarrassed and knew I had to do something. Just then a voice in my head said, "Just speak from your heart Gary." I stepped out from behind the podium and walked in front of it. I began speaking to the audience directly from my heart. I talked about how our lives truly cannot begin until we learn to forgive ourselves and by doing so forgive others. I was speaking the words, "Unconditional love is what we all seek." when the bedside alarm clock went off, it was 3 a.m. With a rhythmic jolt of unexpected noise, I jumped out of bed, saw the time and said, "Oh my God, the maid must have accidentally set the alarm!" My heart was pounding in my chest. Steve was up but disoriented and I quickly yanked the alarm clock plug from the wall to silence it. I took a deep breath, got back into bed and started sharing my dream in vivid detail with Steve. As I was describing it he sat up, grabbed my arm and looked at me with wide eyes and said, "Oh my God Gary, I was there. I was in the audience." My hair stood on end and I knew without a doubt that this was my confirmation. Sufian's book was truth. If a shared dream were not confirmation enough, then nothing would be.

"Thoughts are more powerful than you ever imagined."

As I began to further understand and witness the power of thoughts, it became clear to me that I was responsible for creating some of the discord that was happening in my work life. The law of attraction teaches that if I AM having negative thoughts about something, then I will draw that very thing to me. I seemed to be amplifying people's bad behaviors by having negative thoughts about those very behaviors. For three nights straight, I was waking up tossing and turning in bed while perseverating on the drama at work. One morning around 3 a.m. (yes, 3 a.m.) I was wide-awake and thinking how nice it would be to leave my job and move to Maui. My mind was flitting from thought to thought and at one point I started thinking about snakes and how much I dislike them. Just another positive reason to move to Maui, there are no snakes and that along with the warm ocean and weather make it a perfect place to live. But then I started thinking about people who might smuggle in poisonous snakes via planes and boats and release them into the wild. I thought of the deadly poisonous Fer-de-Lance snake that bit a TV producer causing him to lose his leg and nearly lose his life. I imagined how awful it would be to have snakes in Hawaii; it would no longer be the paradise I dreamed of living in. I could hear Steve next to me stirring in his sleep and with a loud and slurred yell of terror he woke up. I asked, "Are you okay?" he replied, "I just had a dream that I was bitten by a snake." Could it be a coincidence? I say no. I believe it was just another confirmation of the power of our thinking. It wasn't long after this that a snake found it's way into my house and came slithering through my kitchen door. In the seven years I have lived here, there has never before been a snake seen.

The power of thought may be much more than you think. It's the actual spark of creation. Imagine if you can cause the person next to you to have a nightmare by thinking about something bad, how does this translate to our everyday lives?

"Hearts are for those who live forever."

I think of the heart as both physical and emotional, the heart that keeps us alive and the heart that holds infinite love. It is the organ that pumps blood and oxygen across the roads and highways of our internal universe. Through the veins and arteries, it nourishes the life of every living cell within the biosphere of our structure. This microscopic and unseen world is not unlike the stars and planets in the infinite universe, vast and sometimes incomprehensible. I see the heart as the power plant of this universe. A place where our emotions flow and love permeates. Life cannot exist without it pumping in our chests and therefore we cannot humanly feel or experience love in its absence. When we love or feel emotion for another, our hearts may race, pound, skip and flutter. Whatever the connection is, one fact remains, without a heart, we do not exist in body and neither does the infinite universe in which it gives life and love.

What does love feel like? Is it an intense desire, an unbearable ache, a pounding heart, an adrenaline rush of passionate feelings, the warmth you feel by being around someone? The answer is probably different for everyone. I could never seem to understand the concept of love. It remained a mystery to me for of most my life. Trying to comprehend love and then making it unconditional was exhausting. I was on a plane flying home from Hawaii when I received the gift of understanding for the first time in my life what love is to me. It was late in the evening, my seat back was reclined, the air was smooth, the cabin lights were off and only the reading light of a passenger several rows in front of me was lit. I was listening to Peter Gabriel's instrumental version of San Jacinto and thinking about my life. My head was flooded with memories of current friends, past friends, people no longer living, places I have been and those I long to go to. Feelings were fluid as my thoughts changed. San Jacinto is a stunning song and there is a section where the mood passionately builds and violins begin to soar. Just at the crescendo my father popped into my head and the beauty of the music and the love I felt was so intense that my heart burst open and tears began to spill out of my eyes. Tears of joy, laughter, pain, sorrow and happiness all at once; tears spilling out from the beauty of the music and the loving thought of my father. It was then I realized something. Tears are love in pure liquid form.

So what does it mean to love one's self unconditionally? For me it's a process of learning to forgive every perceived guilt, wrong, flaw or bad thing I feel I have ever done. Never having to think negative thoughts about myself. Accepting my journey without putting limits on it and never having to second guess the things I do. The process is evolving every day. I know that if I cannot love myself unconditionally, then how can I love someone else without conditions? I see many people struggle with giving or receiving unconditional love. There are so many fighting emotions surrounding it. But I do believe we can evolve and elevate our consciousness enough to learn how. I believe that we inherently love ourselves unconditionally. It is in our DNA and our divine birthright. Life's experiences may damage this love, but we can find and activate it again if we are mindful to do it. We can spend our whole lives not believing we are worthy of love, but I believe if you can cry, you can feel its incredible depths. It was through tears that the miracle of love came alive for me. Perhaps if we forgive ourselves we can reclaim that love and acknowledge ourselves as the most powerful creator in our own existence.

"Never allow a person or situation to control your emotions, practice grace."

Everyday I make choices about how I interact with the world and react to my life. While today I make healthier choices, for years I was in a cycle of reacting to situations in an emotional way and surrounding myself with negativity without realizing it.

Every morning I would wake up and the first thing I would do is reach for my iPhone and tap into the news. Without fully realizing it, this would start my day with a big dose of negativity. An executive manager once told me, "You have to know what is going on in the news if you're going to be a strong leader." Since I respected her, I got into the habit and would talk about it with anyone who would listen. Sometimes I would react to the news physically and emotionally like it was happening to me personally. I would get sick to my stomach, angry, frustrated and sometimes quietly curse or gasp at my phone. With each horrible story, some part of me felt I should be doing something, but all I could really do is voice my opinion at lunch or over coffee, "How can this be? Who would do that? My God, this is a sick world. Have we lost all value for human life? Can you believe this is happening?" I kept checking for updates throughout the day. CNN and Facebook were running on my smart phone 24/7 feeding me more negative news. Banners flashed across my screen and I couldn't wait to read the latest headline.

When I arrived at work the day would begin with staff and customers lined up at my office door ready to deliver the problem of the moment. Meeting after meeting was scheduled to discuss issues. More problems arrived via phone calls and emails; many times from unrealistic people who chose to be mean spirited and downright hateful. I would say, "Where is the decency and goodness in people today? Nothing I do seems to be good enough. These people need a reality check."

Sometimes the condescending tone or the unfairness of someone's expectations would send me over the edge and my heart would pound in my chest and my mouth would dry out all the while groveling and apologizing for his or her experience and hoping they couldn't tell I was affected by their rude behavior. I could feel my blood pressure rise and stress hormones release into my body like toxic waste. I had many sleepless nights tossing and turning while perseverating over the negative issues of the day. Because I couldn't sleep, I'd pick up my phone and tune into more bad news. It was a vicious cycle.

I believe my story is somewhat typical. Is it any wonder why the world exists in the state it does? In the law of attraction it states that what we put out, we get back. I couldn't see that the more negative things I concentrated on, the more I drew them into my life. If I spent my night thinking negative thoughts, of course I would find more negativity in the morning, afternoon and evening. I looked for it. If that's all I'm thinking about, that is all I'm going to see and attract. Is it any surprise that as a society, we have perpetual bad news? Much of the world runs on negative fuel because this is all there is at the filling stations. The antidote for me was to choose a different filling station.

As I began to read and understand more about the ramifications of the energy I was putting out and what I was attracting back I started trying things to see if it created different results. Of course it did. I started to be mindful of what I was tuning into. I decided I would only surround myself with positive people and things. No more news, no more taking things personally. I became an observer of situations and detached myself from negative emotions. I began to listen more, talk less and really try to understand and tune into where someone was coming from. I quickly realized that most reactions had absolutely nothing to do with me and I didn't have to fix them or feel bad about it. Most times my intuition would steer me to the truth. Once I stopped owning someone else's negative emotions and experiences, I was free.

I had to ask myself, "Why am I watching the news?" In most instances, there really wasn't anything I could do to change the outcomes and the truth was that the news was used to fuel morbid curiosity about someone else's pain. Unless I was willing to go and fight for every cause presented, all I was doing was stuffing my head full of negativity. When I pondered the question, "Is there really anything I can do about it?" and I answered truthfully, "No." I didn't have to let it affect me anymore nor did I need to continue watching it every day. I believe that when we remove the negative influences in our life whether it is the news, people or situations and chose our well-being first, we begin to create a positive and more peaceful existence. If I don't get involved with negative energies, then I don't have to experience that negativity nor will I attract it to me. If I chose to surround myself with positive people and enlightened souls, then I too will become more positive and enlightened. We become what we surround ourselves with. As I filled my tank with positive fuel I started seeing immediate results. I could clearly see negative fuel for what it was and I no longer needed it. While I do have to live in this world and work in sometimes stressful situations I never forget that I AM the most powerful creator in my universe and I can create my experience with every step I take. I choose how I react to every single situation and the outcome is ultimately in my hands. I meditate daily and create a space where I can stay centered as I watch life unfold in front of me. Since I have learned to still my mind and be a silent observer, I can now watch as others swim in the murky water learning what is needed from each and every encounter in the hardest way while realizing that this lesson isn't for me. Today I chose to be positive and loving.

"Let me take care of me so that I may take care of others."

For many years I either learned or through karma manifested a life of putting others first, being co-dependent, tuning into negativity and amplifying it, but mostly never taking time to nurture my soul. I did it without even knowing. I didn't know what I didn't know and life has a way of setting things up perfectly so the lessons come at just the right time.

I put myself in the role of taking care of others and then not taking care of myself. I see many people do the same thing. We might see ourselves as the caring husband, wife, mother, father, friend, son or daughter. We slip into our roles so easily and believe it is who we are, what we must do and all there is to life. We may even lose ourselves completely and in the process become resentful not always understanding why. We can't grasp what we really want or why we feel the way we do. We just know we don't feel good. A typical day may play something like this: jolted awake by an alarm clock, rush to get ready for work, make coffee, do chores around the house, get the kids ready for school, feed the pets, drive in bumper to bumper traffic and take calls on the way to work so you can get a jump start on the day when you arrive. Each second of our waking state so far is purpose and action while our mind is flitting from one thought to another. What sort of thoughts are we thinking? Are they loving and positive, negative and angry or both? We may spend our entire day trying to help co-workers resolve problems, fielding difficult questions, taking complaints, answering problem-related emails and phone calls. We sometimes commiserate and feel we are not making a difference and just try to keep our head above water. We get frustrated by people's behaviors and need to vent to someone about them. Sometimes there is negative self-talk, "I can't seem to do anything right. I'm useless, boy am I stupid." We get home and find there is still more to do. When and if we finally get to relax we may find ourselves watching TV or stressing out about the news, a drama, or reality show. Without even realizing it, we have been inundated with negativity all day long, don't process it or put it in perspective and we begin to think that this is just the way life is. What if living in this state just creates more of the same and this is a cycle we have created? Maybe it is time to stop and think, how can I break it and start a new one? For me it started by being mindful and learning to recognize when I tune in and tune out. When I identified the cycle, I could then be mindful of the energy I was surrounding myself with. I began to consciously create a different game plan for the day, going to bed earlier, waking up to peaceful music, creating a habit of meditating every morning for at least 20 minutes. I exercised, ate healthier, listened to soothing music on the way to work, stopped taking calls and began living in a state of gratitude for everything in my life. I began looking at all the issues of the day with compassion, unconditional love and understanding and without judgment. I changed my thinking about issues and started seeing the lessons in them not only for myself, but also for others. Instead of being angry or upset I would stop, breathe and have a talk with myself, "Why are you so angry, is this about you or them? Is it personal or just their pain? I don't have to own this, I can observe and choose surrender, acceptance and detachment, compassion and love." I consciously try to see the emotion, lesson and reason behind every behavior and action. This new way of thinking has changed my life and opened my heart to unlimited love and happiness. I choose happiness over anger, love over pain. Until I took the time to take care of myself, I often failed at truly caring for others. Although I was earnest in my attempts, it was often riddled with traces of resentment, expectation and conditions. The first thing I practice every morning is meditation. No matter where I AM this is my priority. It's time to change my thinking, cleanse my mind and connect to the Source. This allows me to be mindful in creating my existence. Miracles happen every day and magnify the synchronicities of our experience. Doubt has been replaced with unshakable knowing. The more love I give myself, the more love is manifested in my life. I try to stay mindful and present for each moment and live in a state of unconditional love and gratitude.

I AM aware of negative self-talk and immediately stop it in its tracks. I replace negative thoughts with positive ones. As I look in the mirror each day I accept myself with the face I have, the body I AM in and forgive myself for anything wrong others or I have done. I remind myself that I AM not perfect but I AM given the ability to love and to forgive and the most important place to start is with me.

Each morning during meditation I repeat, "I AM love, I AM light, I AM happy, I AM healthy, I AM the Resurrection and Light" This is the gift I give myself every day.

"Watching sports is to distraction as unconditional love is to truth-seeking."

From a spiritual perspective, what is the purpose of distraction? I believe it is divinely created to keep us from taking care of ourselves emotionally, physically and spiritually. It is here to keep us out of balance and we need it in order to learn, grow and ultimately, expand our consciousness. I believe that whether in this incarnation or another, our souls eventually elevate. Distractions are tempting and effective in keeping us from being intimately connected with ourselves. How many times have you heard or maybe yourself said, "I don't want to think about anything, I just want to do something mindless." Enter the distractions, which are too many to count. We might spend the day thumbing through magazines, reading a book or watching television. I have recently been thinking about two very powerful distractions: football and television. They are both brilliant creations. Football is so powerful a force that it draws millions of people around the globe to follow it. Many friends tell me it is their favorite pastime, a sweet reprieve from the stresses of everyday life and the best way to socialize with family and friends. Just the other night over dinner an acquaintance and huge sports fan was gushing about her favorite team when I asked her the question, "What is it about football that you love so much?" the answer, "I like rooting for my team, I like it when they win, it feels good, I don't know, I just like it." I have seen it incite jubilation, anger and violence and even drive a man to murder. During a soccer game in Brazil a referee who made an unpopular call on the playing field was brutally stabbed to death by fans. Some people spend hours following the strategy, plays and players, thinking and betting on the odds with fantasy football. Some can allow a sports outcome to ruin their entire day.

Television shows allow us to escape the realities of our own lives by living vicariously through make-believe, drama or supposed reality. I have read articles where reality TV shows' cast members report that the networks want you to think the shows are real, but in reality they are scripted to pump up the drama. It seems that the more drama, the more people watch it. I have seen the bad behaviors on these shows being glorified and then reenacted by people in real life as if they are fashionable. At breakfast, lunch and dinner we talk about our shows and who was killed or kicked off and give our opinions on each character. We judge and condemn while we eat our food and eagerly await the next episode so we can have more to talk about. Escapism is intoxicating. We seek anything and everything that will take our minds off of an intimate relationship with each other and ourselves. By doing this we elude mindfulness, the one thing that will bring us true happiness and unconditional love. I have incited arguments and anger at the very suggestion that television or sports may be mindlessness vs. meditation or truth-seeking is mindfulness. I only try to illustrate that lasting purpose and happiness in life will most likely come from the latter. So I leave it open for you to explore what the purpose of distractions are in your life.

While I have to live and work in this world, I try to limit the doses of negativity and not read or watch too much news, sports, or television. I spend a lot of time thinking about the meaning of life, God, unconditional love and find ways to nurture my soul. The more I focus on spiritual enlightenment and exercise my mind with meaningful books, meditation and nature, the less I fit in. I find myself sitting at the lunch table, out with friends or at a party not really relating the same way I used to. I find that not many people at work and few in my personal life are comfortable with talking about the path to spiritual enlightenment. I have been told that sharing my experiences is weird and not to do it lest people think me crazy. Perhaps our spiritual journey is one we ultimately take alone.

Distractions seem to be filler along the way and at any time we can chose to see them for what they are and jump off the bandwagon into another way of seeing and thinking.

What if we limit or stop allowing negativity and distractions from entering our lives and we replace them with spiritual mindfulness? Instead of turning on the TV, we turn within. Would mindfulness illuminate the path we are destined to find? Instead of being influenced by negative people and energies, what if we surrounded ourselves with love, light and positive influences? I can say with certainty that a whole new life will emerge. I have witnessed it. When I put myself in a space of positivity, I attract more of it to me. As I learned to turn inward and be an observer, I began to understand the importance of each moment, thought and act. If in these I gave unconditional love, I could see the most magical thing begin to happen. I started receiving it back and it was clear that beyond being witness, I was being creator of the most powerful force in our universe. When I move through life observing without judgment, I can see the laws of our existence at work. It becomes clearer why I AM here and placed into each and every situation. There is a purpose to our existence here and the moment we get confirmation, and one day we all do, we will never see things the same way. Synchronicities will reveal themselves everywhere and what was once unreal or uncanny will become common. We will begin to know why every single thing happens in our life and the time frame for understanding will go from years to months, months to days and days to instants. We start this journey by picking out a path with the least distractions. We must consciously seek to eliminate negativity. I believe the answers to all our questions are programmed into our DNA. We only have to activate it by turning our search inward to the God we are, the most powerful creators in the universe.

> **"After the battle, amongst the ruins you will find a tiny spark of light, which is the God that you are. Nourish it and watch it grow."**

It was easy to say, but harder for me to understand that every single struggle I've encountered in this life was for a reason, came at the perfect time and with a gift attached. I have recently found this notion challenged on social media with a backlash of anger. While it may not hold true for everyone, it certainly does for me. It wasn't until I began to study the principles of St. Germain and the *I AM Discourses* that I could see that at the end of every devastation in my life was a tiny spark of light. This light, no matter what the lesson, could never be put out because it was God, the infinite in my immortal soul. The *I AM Discourses* taught me that I AM God, the most powerful creator in the universe. They taught me the power in two words: I AM. Whenever I say the words, "I AM" I AM invoking God. If I say, I AM happy, then I AM. Just the same as if I say I AM sick, I AM. I use affirmations such as I AM happy, I AM healthy, I AM love and not I AM tired, I AM sick, I AM sorry. The discourses enlightened me that in order to manifest good things in my life I must be in alignment with my higher God self. Through the tears and the hardest of times and losses, no matter what this tiny spark of I AM Light remained. At times the spark was a break in the tears and a moment of clarity, other times it was someone reaching out at the right moment to hold me, let me cry on their shoulder and tell me everything was going to be all right. These moments saved my life and put me in a place to heal and grow in ways I would only later realize. The spark that told me to breathe and kept my heart pumping when I thought I would die would one day activate my divine DNA and allow me to see eternity and to feel unconditional love. This tiny little spark that transcended particles allowed me to see inside people's minds, be in the right place for magic things to happen, like share a dream, battle a dark shaman, invoke a nightmare while giving me amazing confirmations of truth and grace in near death experiences. It has been more than a miracle, it is God screaming, "Hey, Gary, right here, I'm right here!"

I spent most my life thinking that God was outside of me. A grandfather looking figure sitting on a throne in the sky living in an imagined world called heaven full of mansions and angels. This God judged my every move and punished me for every wrong. But once I realized I AM God, we are all God, I could feel and truly believe in the power we have to create our own existence. It was I that guided my destiny, it was I that consoled myself, it was I that was in contact with every particle of light in the universe and all I had to do was sit in stillness long enough to know it. The Masters have been trying to tell us for millennia, but religion has corrupted the message. Imagine if religion taught us the whole truth about God? Would it lose control over us while fear gives way to empowerment? Perhaps it is by divine plan that we have religion if only to stop ensuing chaos. Whatever the reason, I firmly believe that the difference between spirituality and religion is that religion is another person's experience of God. Spirituality is our own. While we live in an ego-driven corrupt world where power and control reigns supreme, remember that nobody can control you. You are the most powerful creator in the universe. You have the ability to create anything you want. God self-realization is the most important thing we can achieve and is essential in manifesting the life we want.

"Although you may not see or feel it, the world operates in perfect balance."

I always believed the idea that if I lived in a perfect world, I would be happy, healthy and everything would go exactly the way I wanted. What I didn't realize was that I was already living in a perfect world and that there is an inherent balance to everything in it. One of the laws of our universe is balance. This means that perfection is a matter of how you look at things. While the majority of our filling stations are supplied with negative fuel, equal yet elusive are the positive ones. There will always be sickness with health, good with bad, light with dark, starving with satiated, tortured with pampered and for every positive a negative. I used to think that my job was to turn someone's negative into something positive, but I learned that not every person experiencing something negative wants to change it. Some people need this experience. It is only when divine DNA is activated that we gravitate toward our true nature. I have been told that I AM a love creature, an entity that has always lived in and gravitated toward the light bringing love wherever I go.

I have learned that I should never try to interfere upon the free will of another. If someone choses darkness, then it is his or her choice. Our choice comes with deciding what we will or will not allow in our lives and what we will create by allowing whatever we decide. Light will go wherever it is allowed, as will darkness.

Whenever we are at our happiest, often something will come along to provide a low. We must experience a low to have a high. You cannot experience happiness unless you have experienced sadness. No matter how sad you are right now; you will feel equal joy on the other side if you are open to it. It's a law of this universe. Once you understand this, the lows are not nearly as low. We have the ability to observe events as a witness and not be sucked into the impending drama and feelings surrounding it. We all can make a choice. When seeing that the world operates in balance, we no longer have to be angry when the weight shifts on the scale. No matter what it is that is happening on this planet, there is an equal and opposite reaction somewhere to balance it. If

I AM laughing right now, somewhere someone is crying, being born and dying, sleeping and waking, starving and eating. This law permeates the entire multiverse. Seek to understand that everything is in perfect balance.

"It is the things that block us that need only forgiveness."

I once knew a woman who was always finding the negative in everything. She was harsh, suspicious, judgmental and hurtful to many people. She called them idiots and imbeciles to their faces and the harder they tried to help her, the meaner she became. She would always find something negative or imagine ulterior motives in most every attempted kindness given to her. Frequently when dining out, she would create a scene embarrassing the servers along with the people she was dining with. Any attempt to correct her complaint only resulted in further anger and insults. It seemed that nothing could satisfy her. Over the course of time I knew her, she experienced one personal tragedy after another. This only compounded the negativity. She was robbed and her anger grew bigger. There was nothing that could be done to comfort her. Her anger escalated to the point that people around her feared for their safety. She refocused her anger on the incompetence of everyone trying to help her, blaming them for her woes. Her disparaging comments and distrust of people continued. With anyone who would listen, she would talk about how awful things were. Approximately five months later, she was diagnosed with cancer. I was saddened at the news. I wondered if her anger was eating her up inside and causing her illness. When I thought she had found peace, something else would infuriate her. Her thinking was consistently unreasonable. I discovered that the more I tried to help her the angrier she became. The more I thought about her negativity, the more she appeared in my life with something negative. When I realized I could not help her, I had to release her from my life. In doing so, I focused on thinking healing and positive thoughts while surrounding her with love. She disappeared from my life peacefully.

There is no judgment in this question and certainly it is not true in every case. Is it possible that her anger created her woes? The law of attraction says that what we put out in energy and thought comes back to us. Is it possible that if we are unkind, uncaring and insulting to people there are unseen forces at work creating consequences?

"I will always trust my intuition."

I have always had a strong sense of intuition and learned over time to implicitly trust it. I have wondered if somehow this gift was activated in my DNA at birth. Whether or not this is a divine gift I do not know. I often experience telepathy, which I believe plays a large role in my intuition. Sometimes when people are telling me something, I can immediately sense if it is not true. Furthermore I can usually see the scene like a movie in my head that contradicts what is being said. I nod and agree, but in my heart I know the truth. During times I may probe into a story I AM often met with a momentary flash of fear just under the surface. I never press, but remember. Inevitably I find out days, months and even years later that my intuition was right. Whether someone is dishonest about their real feelings, intent or actions, I accept their words yet know the truth. I have protected myself this way since childhood. I realize that I have to live in this world, but intuition allows me to steer clear from many bad situations or relationships. We can't always be in touch and honest about everything in our lives and everybody has secrets. Sometimes people believe they are telling the truth and are honestly not aware of their real feelings yet. Every person reading this right now can tell at least one story about how they knew something, but didn't trust their intuition and befell to some painful event because of it. Everyone has intuition. There have been times I have strongly sensed things about someone. But having doubts, I'd run it by a friend or two and then doubt myself further when they would tell me I was crazy. In many cases I've been hurt this way when I was right all along.

I knew a man that suddenly appeared in a good friend of mine's life. He was charming, good looking and disarming. Always said the right things and my friend genuinely liked him and would invite him to dinners and parties introducing him to our circle of friends. I knew immediately when I met him he was disingenuous. I sensed an expert acting out a play on a stage to get acceptance, adoration and ultimately some sort of material gain from every relationship he pursued. I felt sad for him, but my friend and others were smitten with him. I kept a healthy distance and was cordial and deflected his attempts to gain closer contact. He figured this out quickly and stopped trying yet continued with the others. One by one the friendships he forged in our circle ended as the disingenuous intent behind his actions unfolded and his true intent was made clear.

If you ever get the sense something isn't right, it probably isn't. If you get the sense someone is lying, they probably are. If out of nowhere you get a gut feeling that someone is talking about you, its likely they are. Thoughts or feelings don't manifest out of nowhere. We learn to doubt our intuition because we feel we are projecting a past experience on something new. Always trust your intuition.

"You have to believe, never stop believing."

The road to enlightenment is exciting and wondrous. If you truly take the time to nurture and grow your higher self, the rewards are magic. With each book I read and deep meditation I have, I'm drawn into a higher state of consciousness and closer to understanding who I AM and why I AM here. I have learned to accept myself as the I AM presence. I've come to believe that when I say I AM what follows, I AM that. I have learned to become less irrational and emotional and more graceful. I AM an observer with an armor of understanding. But, I AM also human and at times I regress and get pulled into the negative. I slide back into old routines, stop reading, waste time on the Internet and sometimes forget where I've come from. After all I've learned and experienced around self-awareness, the *I AM Discourses* and the law of attraction, I sometimes wonder; what if everything I have experienced is just coincidence and everything I believe to be miraculous is nothing more than a belief without proof? I think it is human nature to question ourselves especially when we live in a world that doesn't always nurture spiritual growth beyond the restraints of traditional religions. My doubts are usually fleeting as I reflect on the storybook of my life and the many astounding confirmations. In my truth, there is absolutely no way there is not a magnificent power in the universe that ties us all together. Through particles of light and higher vibration, I was allowed to enter the mind of another human being and see a childhood event unfold in real time, invite someone into a dream and have them sit in the audience while I gave a talk and manifest a snake bite for the dreamer sleeping next to me. There are too many signs and synchronicities for it not to be true. Nobody can convince me differently. Energy does not lie.

It is amazing to me that according to scholars, we have existed for thousands of years yet we have so little knowledge and understanding of how the ancients were able to build and live in spectacular advanced cities. How is it in recent history that we suddenly accelerated our ability to invent technology at light speed? In 40 years science fiction has becomes reality. I remember just a few short years ago when Bluetooth came out for our mobile phones. I was at a good friend's house having a drink and conversation when the two of us looked at each other with our little electronic devices sticking out of our ears and began to laugh, "Remember Star Trek when Lieutenant Uhura pushed the little device in her ear and said, "Captain, you're breaking up!" We would never have believed that was a possibility and here we were with the same device sticking out of our ears. The irony being on many occasions speaking the words, "I can't hear you, you're breaking up." How can we possibly have come from outhouses and the horse and buggy to Apple Facetime on our iPhones in such a short period? Is it the natural progression of man or is it possible that there has been some sort of intervention in our advancement?

"Don't be afraid, speak your truth and be yourself. It's all there in your genetic code."

I have found it hard to find like-minded people to talk to about spirituality. It is one of those forbidden topics along with money and politics. My experience is people prefer to talk about themselves, their jobs, the news, TV shows or problems. Debating opinions is often the flow of conversation. Topics on the paranormal, spirituality and other worldly things are far too often taboo or viewed as fanciful and ridiculous. I believe that divine knowledge is programmed in our DNA and lives in our collective unconscious. While every one of us has the same access, varying degrees of life experience and karma contribute to blocking it. The concept of the individual as God is blasphemous and daunting for many. I have found when I introduce this concept people squirm in their seat or shirk it off. Is belief in ourselves as God any more of a stretch than traditional religion asks of us? Religions dominate the globe and for most people require blind faith. I spent most of my life looking for answers in religion and was always left less than fulfilled and with more questions than answers. The concepts introduced to me by the *I AM Discourses* are as ancient as any religion and answered most all my questions. The synchronicities and confirmations I have received have been nothing short of miraculous. I have often asked for confirmations of truth around religion and have never received one. The one universal truth that runs through all religions is unconditional love. Perhaps it is man who always gets in the way of this and the rules that are made up are for his own benefit and to allay his own fears. The message of God is pure yet when filtered by man and religion, becomes corrupt.

"You are the most powerful creator in the universe."

I believe the orgasm is the highest level of physical pleasure we experience in this life. During sex, we conjure up the genetic code of God and call all souls from eternity existing in the stillness to come be on earth. The longing in our bodies, the intense peaks of pleasure for women and for men ending in explosive, hair-raising ecstasy that shoots through his body ushering in millions of souls to fight for their chance to be the one that sparks creation the moment they hit the egg. Of course not all sex creates life, but there is nothing more powerful we can do as creators than to make a human life.

We not only create life, we create our existence and experience with every step we take.

"Remember, you are the light."

In meditation, I close my eyes and still my mind. I have been able to see particles of light since I was a child long before I knew what they were. Many people I have worked with in time have been able to see them as well. If I sit quietly with my eyes closed whether in the dark or light I immediately see little specks of light vibrating with different colors. I behold these molecules and know that they exist everywhere; in the air of the room, in the walls, the chair in which I AM sitting, in space, through every black hole, constellation and dimension in existence. They have always been here and always will be, vibrating the light that makes up everything in our infinite multiverse. I can transport my consciousness anywhere these molecules vibrate for every vibrating molecule of light is connected. Everything is molecules, zeros and ones in a cosmic computer that knows no beginning or end. We are light in genetic code given to us by our creator. I discovered while meditating when I lift my hands up and move them about keeping my gaze on the vibrating light, I was nothing more than a dense mass of energy moving through the space. The vibration of light is always there. It is in us, around us, in every part of our body. We are moving through the vibration together, our souls vibrating in the light particles that form together and make our human bodies.

"Seeking attention outside of yourself is a dead-end street."

Whatever we do and where ever we go, there is attention that we pull to us. If I dress provocatively then chances are I AM seeking sexual attention. If I only hang out with intellectual people, then I probably see myself as an intellectual or I AM hoping to attract intellectual people to me. If I go out to bars, I will probably meet people who like to party. Knowing that I AM a magnet for what I put out is key in understanding how I AM responsible for creating my existence. Where I put my attention, is what I will create. Many people put all of their attention on being seen, heard, accepted and loved. These are universal needs. Many times our ego becomes inflated and these needs become so desperate and demanding that they often dominate our existence. Ego is one of the most powerful forces in the universe. It often shows up when we don't get the desired results we want. If we are trying our hardest to look good and then someone points out our flaws, it can be devastating to ego. Even though flaws are only made noticeable by the expectations that society creates. In the 50s women with full figures were highly desired while today it is slender figures. The opposite can be true. If people are always telling us how great we look or how awesome we are, that can also over inflate ego and create a monster. If am gaining weight or I have a big pimple on the end of my nose, nobody needs to tell me, I'm well aware of it and ego becomes deflated. If I AM spending 12 hours a day at the office and never hear that I AM doing a good job and I AM reminded daily of things I still need to do, ego becomes bruised. If I spend hours preparing a delicious meal and I don't get a thank you, ego becomes hurt. The list goes on. Some may not be seeking attention while others are constantly seeking it. For many the only attention that seems to matter is the bad or the lack of any at all. We tell ourselves that we will lose that extra weight, get back to the gym, try harder, do better and still at the end of the day we don't quite get the attention we seek or think we need. We may start down a path of negative self-talk and we don't even register what we are saying to ourselves. Ultimately we may feel rejected. What we fail to realize is that all the negative thoughts are a self-fulfilling prophecy. As our mind churns, turns and dialogs, we are creating and attracting exactly what we are thinking. Ego is so powerful that it blinds us to the truth behind attention seeking; we are not our bodies, jobs, successes or failures. We are not what other people think about us or how hard we work or how much we give. We are something so much bigger. We are light that shines unconditional love. We learn to shine unconditional love by first loving ourselves. No one else can do this for us. We must see past our need for attention and realize that ego is what keeps us from being in the moment and true enlightenment. In meditation we can look inward and find the things that truly matter. It's already programmed in our DNA. Seek and it will unlock. The greatest gift you will ever receive is the one that you give yourself. It's called unconditional love. By giving it, you will finally begin to attract the things you desire.

"I AM perfect divine interaction when I AM absent of ego."

I know a 90-year-old woman who has been very successful in life. She has received attention and praise for the books she has written and ensuing TV appearances and awards she has won. When I first met her, I knew we had a spiritual connection; one that comes from having lived many lives together. She exudes a magnetic energy that draws people to her. She can quickly disarm a person and make them believe that after one meeting they either are going to be or are already best friends. She gives love and attention to everyone she meets and knows how to meet them exactly where they are. Without conscious awareness, she uses the law of attraction. She has never studied it or read a book about it. She knows it as leftover knowledge from a previous life and has experienced amazing success because of it. I often call her my queen and tell her that she manipulates the universe. She has pulled hundreds of people together, started ventures and think-tanks that have paved the way for many women of her generation and continues to do so today. She has an amazing mind. Her thinking is scientific, yet she passionately seeks to understand the unknown. Her litmus test has always been the scientific method, yet after meeting me and hearing my experiences, she is baffled. For her, the unbelievable synchronistic events, past life recollections and out of body conversations we have shared have awakened something and brought about a shift in her thinking. When we first met she was in therapist mode trying to determine if I was crazy or if there might be some truth to what I was saying. She was intrigued by our connection and the overwhelming attraction. She kept asking me more about my life and the more I shared the more she felt the connection and wanted badly to experience and know the things that I did. A self-proclaimed agnostic and scientist, my views and beliefs were fascinating yet unbelievable to her. She wanted to understand and even more so, she wanted to believe. She started reading books and meeting with me every week. After 90 years, changing her belief system has not been easy. When I told her the first thing she had to do was lose her ego, her face said, "Ego, what ego?" She has lived her whole life in ego and this was hard for her to hear. Ego thinking, "Do you know how successful I AM, maybe I don't need this enlightenment thing!" I told her she had to take all the attention-seeking behaviors, focus her energy inward and accept that she is God. She looked at me, looked down, shook her head side to side and said, "Hmm, God, I'm not sure about that one." Eventually she'd say, "Okay! I'll try. Then came back the next day saying, "You're asking me to be boring, this takes all the fun out of life. I love my life! I'll have nothing to talk about." And then by the end of the conversation she'd be back to, "What do I have to do?"

Spiritual growth and enlightenment is not easy, it's work. For some it seems near impossible and for others it's not even on their radar. But I assume if you are reading this book, it's on yours. When a soul becomes aware, much to ego's chagrin, all the money, success, fame and attention will no longer be enough. She wants spiritual enlightenment and has tested the waters. If nothing else she understands that to have spiritual growth she needs to get out of ego and into meditation. She wants to believe that there she'll find the Source she seeks but she has to want it bad enough to change. To gain spiritual enlightenment, we must lose the ego. She has started the journey at 90.

"I have always been and will always be divine light and love."

When I meditate I close my eyes and repeat the I AM mantras until I connect with I AM God. My mind becomes still and my breath begins to slow. I AM quickly enveloped in light and begin vibrating with the particles in this magical space. Here I AM connected purely to Source by unconditional love. Often tears will fall from my eyes. The energy particles I bathe in vibrate throughout eternity. These dancing sparks are divine light. The endless realm where Source is omnipotent, expanding through every atom of my physical body and through every biological and inanimate structure that exists. It permeates everyone and every thing. It has always been here and always will be. All things simply move through it. Source can take me anywhere in the multiverse. There is no concept of time or space as everything happens simultaneously. Like Source, I AM omnipotent. Light is what holds us together as one. Our souls are part of Source and, as God, we have always been and always will be, either in this human form or another bodiless form.

I believe that when God created human life on this planet, he fused his DNA with ours to make us in his image and to program us with unlimited love and understanding. In more recent times our DNA has activated further to accelerate technological advancement which in turn gives us better understanding of the laws of this universe. Over millennia, humans have continually advanced in many aspects, yet still we continue to struggle with harmony. Distorted ego and ignorance are the last hurdles to lasting peace and love. Until everyone is taught and willing to embrace their true nature of unconditional love we will remain in a cycle of violence, war, terrorism and self-destructive behavior. We must have conscious awareness of the ego's control. Whether it is history, myth, folklore or religion, we are often taught that our proposed creators are wrathful. This is man's interpretation of karma and lack of understanding that he is God himself and that it is he that is wrathful. Many people believe that God lives outside of them with elaborate stories to support it. I believe that all religion is created with elements of truth. Not just one being right and the others wrong. There is a universal message of love in all of them.

There have been many light sources on this planet, Jesus being one that has endured over 2,000 years. However, man's ego and need to control has corrupted his message one way or another so that it is distorted or entirely lost. This holds true for most religions today. You may or may not accept this, but I encourage you to do some research on ancient mythology, folklore and religions. They are all strikingly similar with miraculous tales of flying Gods coming from the stars, benevolent angels, dark spirits and demons, resurrections and miracles. Our modern monotheism has close ties to ancient mythology and cults. This more than gives pause for further reflection. Keep an open mind and frame it within what you feel comfortable. Gods, angels, demons and ghosts are ideas we have come to have faith in, just words with strong associations to them taught to us by religion and sometimes movies and the arts.

Regardless of your beliefs on how we got here or who we are, I believe that one thing is true, this planet is a repeating pattern with its own laws and we are here to learn one thing, divine love. There is a genetic code in everyone that inherently knows this already.

"No matter what horrors you see every day, face them with love."

Anyone who watches the news can see the horrors that go on in the world every day. Terrorism, murders, racism, bullying, plane crashes, disasters, mass graves found, animal torture, molestation, wars and there is no end to it. Throughout our history, the world has been shadowed with darkness. What fate brings those into harm's way while others seem to go throughout life unscathed? Is it a game of Russian roulette? Is it some random computer playing out odds until your number comes up? Do we have any control in our life's experiences?

I interpret my life's ups and downs with a belief that I have some sort of karmic debt to pay. With being bullied in school and every difficulty and heart breaking loss I've experienced, there has been a profound lesson. I have had friends become furious with me over the idea of bad things happening to innocent people. I never assume I know everything about someone and what they should or shouldn't experience. It is not about deserve or not deserve. Karma can be instant or it can carry over from past lives. People protest, "Did that child deserve to be beaten, did that woman deserve to be raped and did that man deserve to die of cancer?" We are furious that a benevolent God could let such terrible things happen. Many believe it is because there is no God at all. I know that God didn't allow any of it. God isn't an entity sitting on a throne in heaven directing who is going to suffer and who is going to have a good time. God is all of us. I AM God and every one of you reading this is God. Aside from natural disasters, humankind is responsible for all the good and evil in the world. Where we are at with our karmic understanding at any given time dictates how we receive things that come to us, good or bad, light or dark, benevolent or evil and whether or not we see that everything happens as it should. From rock to insect, insect to animal, animal to man we have been every design of creation both inanimate and living. Living in our human bodies we are all connected to each other by particles of light and share a collective unconscious. Not every soul is enlightened yet, but it will be. When the pain becomes great enough we either learn or the lessons will continue to repeat themselves, possibly over many lifetimes.

I AM reminded of a video on YouTube where a young man is blindfolded with a sign that says, "I trust you, do you trust me? Hug me." He stands on the sidewalk with his arms out stretched to be embraced. It takes a while yet, in time, there is a line of people waiting to hug him. It is one of the most powerful examples of unconditional love I have seen and reminds me that no matter what horrors we may face in our lives, we must remember to face them with love, blindly with arms outstretched.

"Manage each situation with grace, never let your emotions cause you to fall."

Someone cuts me off in traffic then flips me off. Anger rises, face flushes and heart is pounding in my chest. Do I lose control? What is my first response? With adrenaline pumping through my body, how do I respond with thoughtfulness? We've all lost our cool. It's easy to do, but once it's done, the damage can be lasting and the karmic ramifications binding. We can all learn to respond to anger, disappointment and fear with grace if we learn to play out the tape. If I were vengeful and chased the person down who flipped me off, what good would it do? Would they stop the car and start a fight? If they were in the wrong and they flipped me off to begin with, what makes me think they are in their right mind? Or worse, what if they carry a pistol in their glove box? How many news stories have you seen on road rage and someone getting killed? What if this was my last day on earth because I chose to pursue an angry driver who decided to flip me off because they were in a hurry and I was in their way? What if they were rushing to the hospital to comfort a dying family member? We have a huge responsibility in our reactions. We create our existence with every single step we take. Nothing happens to us, we create it. Is it possible for us to stop and think before we react? Yes we can, we have a choice. We are intelligent beings and we are always able to be kind. Isn't it just as easy to say, "This isn't about me." and let it go?

If my spouse were having an affair, would jealousy or anger do anything to heal my pain? The answer is no. We have absolutely no control over what other people do. We only have control over the way we react. Jealousy is a useless emotion. The key to curing jealousy is in knowing that we are okay alone. If our spouse is flirting, let them flirt. Play out the tape. If we become jealous, they become resentful and there goes intimacy. Who wants to be with a jealous person? It's not very attractive. If they are going to cheat, they are going to do it whether or not we get mad or jealous. Jealousy puts the law of attraction in motion. We worry that our partner is cheating and whether or not they are we are putting it out in the universe and setting the wheels of creation in motion. What you fear you draw to you. If they are innocently flirting and we become jealous, then we will most likely be pushing the one we love away. At the end of the day, if they are cheating, we will survive and we have to trust, it isn't about us. We have to be okay with ourselves first. It doesn't mean we're not going to hurt, it means we'll be okay no matter what, and no matter how painful it is, we will have equal joy and happiness on the other side. That's the way it works. Stay strong, make the choice to observe closely what is happening and the more we think about it, the more we will find the divine plan in everything. If we decide to take the path of jealously, anger or fear, remember the lessons will repeat.

"Do your part everyday to send thoughts of love and peace to the world."

The power of thought is massive, don't underestimate it. Our thoughts are continuously being projected into space via energy transmitted through a hundred billion neurons firing in our brains. It is similar to the way binary code works on a cell phone. Information goes out into space in the form of zeros and ones to a cell tower and is then directed to another phone. The message is transmitted by sound waves, letters and symbols. Your phone conversation stays isolated in a delineated stream of energy so that it doesn't bleed into any other phone calls. If you could see it, it would look like a light saber from Star Wars in a spherical wave. Imagine that if you could see the energy of every single thought in front of your eyes and somehow your brain had the ability to view the energy of spiking neurons as clearly as it can see the pages on this book you are reading, you would see streams of energy unfold before your eyes like a computer matrix of amazing magnitude. It's all there, yet the human eye can't see it. So much of our world and the energy in it is not visible, yet it's all there from the tiniest atoms to grandest waves of energy swimming around us carrying invisible information to the knowing and unknowing. Don't ever think that when you look at someone and make a judgment that they don't feel it. It is transmitted to them and whether or not they are aware of it they get the signal and feel it. It could arrive in a thought such as, that person is staring at me; they think I'm fat or they are attracted to me, whatever it may be. Sometimes the things we think are not really our own insecurities or thoughts, but often times thoughts being transmitted to us by others. If we spend our time thinking about how bad our lives are and how awful the world is, how angry we are about what someone said to us, we are transmitting this energy to whomever and to wherever we are thinking. Think of it as a text message being sent right into the brain of another or into every TV screen in the world. Thoughts are everywhere feeding our subconscious and conscious minds. Be very careful what you are putting out because not only are you transmitting, you are calling upon the law of attraction and will be receiving what you are putting out. If you are judging people for their weight, don't be surprised when one day you have that weight gain yourself. Just as if you are kind and loving and sending those thoughts, the likelihood that you will have others feeling those things about you are very likely. Every day, when you take the time to meditate, be sure to send thoughts of love and peace out into the world. Imagine if everyone on the planet were to do this, surely we would have love and peace on earth.

"We are here to self-actualize then help others; how can I be of service?"

I have spent most of my adult years trying to understand spirituality. Hours researching religion, ancient mythology, evolution and ancient alien theory have taught me one thing; there is truth in all of it. The stories of our origins, evolution and journeys are similar. Researchers continue to be vexed by how closely related architecture, religion and mythology were amongst ancient civilizations. While travel was not possible from Egypt to Mesoamerica, they both shared similar gods and pyramids. There are many theories, but could it be that this is more proof that we all share a collective unconscious and thoughts from one side of the world travel to the other through energy? I believe we should challenge what we are taught. When our head and heart are in alignment, the truth becomes clear.

It is clear to me that any belief that condones murder, violence or oppression is neither of God or Light. I believe religions are often distorted from the original truth that was imparted by the Masters who brought them. Belief systems that profess anything other than unconditional love are corrupted. When I have a doubt about something I have experienced, in meditation I ask Source, "Is this of the truth and light? Send me a sign." Confirmation often comes when my heart and head connect with an overwhelming feeling of unconditional love. Tears will spill out of my eyes from the sheer beauty and gratitude of it. Other times it will come in a dream or incredible synchronicity.

I believe that every soul's journey is different, but ultimately leads to the same place. Some people are living on the streets struggling to find food and a place to sleep, but are happy. Others are born into great wealth, battle drug addiction and are miserable. I believe that no matter where we live or what life we were born into, each of us will one day seek enlightenment. We may not know it now, but eventually we will. It may take lifetimes before we begin a spiritual journey. If sharing our journey helps another person to activate, be grateful. Sharing with others isn't pushing beliefs on them. We are here to be in service to each other. We can't control how people will react to us, but we can control how we react to them. I come from a place of unconditional love; I can lose nothing by doing this.

I ask myself every day how I can be of service. I Give. The more I give, the more I open myself up to receive. I try to never pass up an opportunity to help someone. I try to never walk or drive by a homeless person asking for money on the corner. Before I pull out a quarter from my pocket, I grab a bill and if I have a one, a five and a twenty, I give the twenty if I can. I don't think about how they are going to spend it, I think about love.

"Don't be afraid of your dreams."

When daydreaming we are in an actual state of creation transmitting to the universe the things we desire.

I spent over 15 years of my life focused on the dream of a successful music career. At the time, getting a major label recording contract came with roughly the same odds as winning the lottery. But I never let the odds scare me and I never doubted that my chance would come.

I spent years writing music, performing and recording CDs. I put all my energy into it and truly believed that I had something to share. I played at local clubs and coffee houses almost every night of the week. It was the definition of dynamic volition in motion. I was able to find a reputable studio and record my first self-released CD and was able to get several well-known studio musicians to play on it. I sent this CD to the top entertainment lawyers in the industry looking for representation knowing that I would get a call back. I waited patiently each day as rejection letters came in, until one day I got a call from Owen Sloan. Owen was a successful entertainment lawyer and represented several famous artists. He shared that he had listened to my music, liked my sound and would like to help me get exposure. We set up a meeting at his offices in West Los Angeles and hit it off. He took me out for lunch and laid out a plan to get my music out to his contacts in the industry and ultimately a record deal. I was high on adrenaline. Here I was, now contracted with a top entertainment lawyer and my dream was well on its way to becoming a reality. It took about two months and several rejections before Owen called me and asked, "Do you know David Kershenbaum?" Of course I did, he was responsible for launching the career of Tracy Chapman and worked with Kenny Loggins and many of my favorite artists. He told me that David heard my music and loved it. He wanted to meet with me at his then new label, Morgan Creek Records where he was co-founder and president. Owen told me he wanted me to come with just my guitar. I was elated. I shared the news with all of my friends and I knew without a doubt that this was my big break. I visualized that I would be playing alongside Tracy Chapman, maybe opening up for her. I practiced several of my songs in preparation for our meeting. The day I walked in his office and saw the platinum albums of Tracy Chapman on the wall, I knew I had arrived and my destiny was staring me in the face. I introduced myself, we made some small talk, then sat down on two white leather sofas right across from each other. He asked me what I wanted from my music and I told him, "If I can move someone with my music, then I have been successful." He asked me to play a couple songs. Here I was sitting on a sofa in David Kershenbaum's office, eyes closed and singing my heart out to one of the most successful music producers of our generation. When I opened my eyes, I could see him sitting across from me with his eyes closed. After the second song, he opened his eyes and the first words out of his mouth were, "Gary, the world needs to hear your music." I nearly started crying, but held it in. This was it. It was just as I imagined. We said goodbye and he told me he would be reaching out to Owen in the next couple of weeks for next steps. I went home and shared my good news with friends, family and my then partner. Everyone was excited. I was on such a high, I don't think my feet touched the ground for a week. I was grateful and in my meditations I thanked God every day. At the same time this dream was clearly becoming a reality, an element of fear was born. It started the day my partner uttered the words, "Now you're going to be famous and leave me." I laughed it off, "Of course I'm not. I don't want this dream without you." He said it again, "No, you're going to leave me." I started to play those words over and over in my head. I thought, if I do get famous, I'd be thrust into the limelight, people will find out I AM gay and it would be the end of my career. My childhood fears and wounds started playing like a movie in my mind. I couldn't imagine how this would play out in a public way. It was a much different world in the 80s and gay musicians were not looked upon favorably in the entertainment industry. My partner would have to live in the shadows and I would have to live a lie. I had already decided that my friend Lorraine would be "the woman in my life" and would be my cover. This was a sad reality. I started to play out the tape of being on the road with all the attention and what would it do to my relationship and what if I were found out for who I really was? For the first time I started to have fears and doubt. I began to think about how it could possibly destroy my life. My excitement was now mixed with fear. In the back of my head, I knew that my success could be my downfall and my relationship's failure. I was already sabotaging my success by putting out this negative energy. Despite these fears, I tried to remain optimistic, yet grew worried when I didn't hear back from David for one, two then three weeks. Each time I would call Owen I would hear, "I'll try and reach out again, I don't know what is taking him so long, he was so excited after meeting with you." It was almost a month later that Owen called and told me, "David decided to pass on you at this time. Morgan Creek isn't in the position to invest a million dollars on an unknown artist. They told me to keep them appraised of your progress." I was devastated. How could this be? He said the world needed to hear my music. How could this momentum build to such a frenzy only to fizzle in the end? Today I can clearly see why. When I started projecting fear, everything changed. My fear of being found out as a gay man was so intense that I believe David picked it up as I broadcasted it loudly to the universe. Not that he thought I wasn't worth the investment; the universe protected us both. A million dollar investment on an unknown gay man spelled certain failure.

This probably was not a lesson that David or I needed to learn in this life. I could never have lived with myself knowing that I was responsible for a new record company failing because of my lie. I do believe that at that time, being outed as a gay artist would have led to instant failure and possible financial ruin for the label.

In 2000, I started watching the television show Survivor. After hearing the announcement for contestants to apply for season two I decided, here's a final chance to have my music heard. It was a different time and things had changed significantly for gay people since the 80s and after-all the winner of season one was openly gay. It seemed that everyone on the show was getting huge press just for being cast and became celebrities just by being on the show. My thought was that if I could get cast, I could have 15 minutes in the limelight and I would get the exposure I needed for my music to be heard. Again, dynamic volition took hold and I began to imagine myself on the show, winning the show and having my music finally get momentum. I made a video of myself playing my guitar and talking about my life. I learned from news sources that over 60,000 contestants had applied to be on the show. It didn't stop me from believing that I would be chosen amongst the thousands. I meditated on it every day and waited knowing that I was going to be contacted. Sure enough, several weeks later I received a phone call that floored me. I had been chosen to move forward in the interview process. A few weeks later I was off to Hollywood for an in-person audition. I spent the better part of a day being asked a series of crazy questions to delve deep into my thinking. After a casting director pointed out a very handsome man in the room, she asked if I would sleep with him, and if I were chosen for the show, would I try? I immediately responded, "Absolutely not, I'm in a monogamous relationship." I sensed she was hoping for a different answer. When asked what I would bring on the show, I said my guitar so I could bring music to everyone. Out of 60,000 applicants, I made it to the final 20 people. The audition lasted a few hours and I was given a confidentiality agreement to sign that stated I would not speak to anyone about the show or my auditions or I could be liable for millions of dollars in damages. I was allowed to ask my place of employment for the time off should I be chosen and other than that, I couldn't talk to anyone about it. I was told to pack a bag and be ready to go at any time. I could be receiving a call and had to be ready to walk out the door in less than 20 minutes. I went home elated then began the slow ticking clock of waiting for that call. After the audition, I began to second-guess the way I answered several of the questions. Maybe I should have been more racy. Instead I was true to myself. Several weeks went by and every time the phone would ring my heart would pound. One day, I received a call and recognized the casting director right away. She said, "Gary, I just wanted to let you know that the whole team loved you, but we decided not to chose you this season, please reapply." From the ensuing conversation I was able to ascertain that since they had a gay character on the first season, they were not going to have one this time. I was their gay character. I believe they would have cast me anyway if I were open to being the gay man who tried to seduce the straight men on the show. I wouldn't be that character. Again, I was at the precipice of getting my music exposed. But, I clearly understand why it didn't happen and I AM grateful for being true to myself.

I always wanted fortune more than fame so I could live the life I desired. Lorraine and I had a dream to visit Paris together one day. I always told her that when I made it big I would take her, buy her a fancy dress and we would sit at an outdoor café and watch the people walk by. It always brought a smile to our faces. After years of searching for Lorraine, it was a heartwarming surprise when she called me out of the blue one day while I was traveling in Europe. Sadly, her speech was slurred, but she said, "See honey, you are living your dream." only the tape played out differently. I was able to create everything I wanted without my music or compromising myself or anyone else. In many ways I AM grateful that my music career didn't take off. Everything happened perfectly.

If you have a dream, don't let fear destroy it. The most beautiful thing you can do is to be true to yourself. Trust that everything has a way of leading you where you need to be.

"If unconditional love is not enough, then let them go with love and light."

I have learned many lessons about loving and letting go. People are here to accompany me, I do not own, control or have any power over them. Most importantly, I cannot pick or chose whom I love or who loves me.

Have you ever been madly in love with someone that didn't feel the same about you? You spend your waking hours thinking about them, doing things to get them to notice you and look for ways to bring them happiness even at the expense of your own. Eventually you find out they just aren't into you. The answer is simple; doesn't matter how good looking, how successful or how willing you are, you can't make someone desire you if they don't. It's a universal law. Romantic love and sexual attraction are often reserved for life's lessons. When I started to understand the spiritual meaning of love I began to find that sexual attraction and the needs I projected on people were all about me and not them. I had to love myself first before I could be loved or truly love another.

There always came a time in my failed relationships when I realized that they were no longer working. The constant arguing, dwindling lack of things in common, growing in different directions, dishonesty, infidelity, loss of physical attraction, resentment and boredom all played a part. And then there were times I knowingly accepted these things because I believed there wasn't anything better out there. Good relationships do not exist without unconditional acceptance and love. If we are going to spend our lives intimately with another, we better get used to the idea. How many of us take the time to really think about what we want in a partner before we start looking for one? Do we sit down and write out a list of attributes, must haves and deal breakers? In my early relationships I never thought a thing about it. It was full speed ahead with general attraction, sometimes growing into infatuation and ultimately them liking me more than I did them and me staying because I was co-dependent. I repeatedly didn't trust my intuition and each time I was reminded why I should. In my early relationships I overlooked all the red flags, forgave all the shortcomings, bad behaviors, infidelities, lies and turned my back on my God-given intuition and tried earnestly to help them change. I can laugh about it now, but I really thought I could change someone. All I had to do was use guilt, control and threats. I spent futile months and years doing this until I had to accept there are things I had no power to change. I had to decide what I was willing to live with and things that I was not. It was my choice and mine alone. I learned after two failed relationships that I should make a list of all the things I wanted from a partner before I started dating again. After all, it couldn't hurt, and a therapist friend told me it was a good idea. It started simple. Must have a job, a past relationship that lasted at least two years, a good relationship with parents, a car, a place to live other than with parents, a kind heart, a caring soul, a sensitive person, must be good with people and animals, must treat waiters with kindness and respect and lastly, no sex for at least 6 weeks. (Starting relationships with sex never worked for me.) I started dating several people; one by one they all fell by the wayside as I held fast to my list. Most couldn't make it through the first three items. After several months, I finally found the one that met all the criteria. Beautiful thing is, 21 years later we are still together. Why has this relationship been successful? Because if you have the basic fundamentals checked off your list, and you make a choice to accept the person for whom they are and love them unconditionally, you can survive anything. If unconditional love isn't enough and your lives begin to go in different directions and you or they need to leave for whatever reason, go with love and light because no matter what, you are going to be okay.

"We have arrived at our destination, let the love shine through."

This whisper came just short of a month into my journey. I knew that I wanted to write a book; I just didn't know how I was going to put it together and what the message was going to be. I did know three things, one that I could create the life I wanted, two I could chose the people I wanted in my life and three, I could connect to the Source every day and gain wisdom and insight. The whisper came after a deep meditation where I expanded my light big as the sun then exploded it out to eternity. I could feel every molecule that connects everything together and there in that space was stillness and the one thing I have been searching for my entire life, unconditional love. It was magnificent like a sea of warm golden light permeating every particle of my existence. I had arrived at my destination, discovered a path directly to the Source where I could just be and let the love shine in. Tears came pouring out my closed eyes with each breath for when with the Source, nothing else in life can compare to its sheer beauty.

"What will you be?"

What do you want your life to look like? Do you want to write a book? Climb Mt. Everest? Live a long life? Have a supportive partner? Have children? Create a lifetime of amazing memories? Do you want to live beyond the day-to-day and seek to understand your higher purpose?

Most of us never take the time to map out our goals because we feel like a hamster in a wheel. Our lives go on autopilot and years fly by. I think of the movie *Boyhood*. It's a simple yet compelling look at winging life and the process of growing up for both parents and children. The story follows a family over the course of 12 years. The mother spends all her time trying to make a better life for her family. She has two children, three failed relationships, goes back to school, graduates, gets a good job, buys a house and all the while her children are growing up and apart from her. In the end, when her son leaves the house to go to college she breaks down and cries because she feels the only thing left is death. Unless you are willing to think about what you want from life and create your destiny, you'll get exactly what is coming and you may not like it. Don't wait until the end and say I wished I would have. Map out your life, make goals, create a list, check it daily and manifest your dreams. Celebrate the successes when they arrive and experience the triumph of making it happen. You have the power to make anything happen. Never forget that.

"Stop and pause, how did I make them feel?"

One of the first things I was told about feelings is that I wasn't powerful enough to make anyone feel anything and that people are responsible for their own feelings. However, I don't believe it entirely. In every interaction we have, there is an opportunity to send loving energy and create an atmosphere that fosters good feelings. Have you ever had a conversation with a friend or loved one where you told them, "You're beautiful, I love you!" and have it turn out bad? While we are not in control of another person's feelings, we are in control of the energy we bring to the equation. I AM often speaking to groups of people and before I begin, I scan the room and try to make eye contact with each person and genuinely acknowledge their presence. If I show up with thoughts in my head about what I'm going to talk about, the point I want to make and take my focus off the people, then I tune out of the energy and life force in the room. This does two things: people are less interested in what I AM talking about and they are much less engaged.

When we see past all the issues, points and circumstances and tune into the connection and light we all share, the undeniable truth becomes clear, that unconditional love is the only thing that matters. By connecting to each soul with loving thoughts, eyes and light, we activate something that can't be seen or heard. It is an energy created on a particle level that transmits and permeates every single thing. It is the acknowledgment of being that we all share. When you get into this thought pattern you will notice things differently. Mostly, people are tuned out from the energy in a room and deeply immersed in their emotions and thoughts. They are not aware of their I AM presence. If we persist in sending unconditional love, we may see some people feel uncomfortable and not quite knowing why. They don't know how to receive it because they don't feel it for themselves. Have you ever seen that uncomfortable look someone gets when they are insecure about something? It appears as if they want to crawl out of their skin. It may have been prompted by a judgmental or hurtful thought that you or someone around you is sending. People feel energy and thoughts are very powerful. I recently read an article about a heavy-set man at a concert in London who was having a great time dancing. A group of people started watching him and rather than send love, smile and be happy at his joy, they laughed and snapped photos. But the cruelty didn't stop there; they posted two of the photos online with the caption of, "Spotted this specimen trying to dance the other week. He stopped when he saw us laughing". One photo showed the man happy and dancing and the other of him shamed and looking down sadly. The hurt caused by this single incident goes beyond the victim. It will be equally hurtful and damaging to those who laughed and posted the photos. They have no idea that the hurt they caused will now come back to them one way or another. Things like this happen every day. This man deserved to be loved and encouraged to have fun. Our outer shells mean nothing. This man is you. This man is your other God self. Next time you start to judge, remember, you are judging yourself. Remember to always send unconditional love, for that, you can lose nothing. After the story hit social media it spurred an outcry and rally of support. Celebrities and others decided to throw a huge dance party and made him the guest of honor. For in the moment of embarrassment and shame he felt it united our hearts and souls. We began to connect and protect him with love and unconditional acceptance. This is progress. I imagine that the people involved in posting the original photos and comments have suffered equally, if not more.

"You can have everything you want."

You can have everything you want, just don't think it will be in the exact package you imagined.

Did anyone ever tell you that you can't always have everything you want? The seed of this is often planted when we are young and developing. Perhaps in was in the toy isle at the grocery store when you wanted that shiny new toy and your mother said no and through your tears she said, "You can't have everything you want." As we grow up we hear it over and over until it finally becomes a reality that we accept as truth. It wasn't until the book *The Secret* introduced the ancient law of attraction to the masses that people began to understand the power of manifestation.

If we retrace the steps of our life in intricate detail, we will begin to see how our thoughts, feelings and actions played a big part in everything we have achieved. From 12- to 15-years-old I experienced life in a small rural town with a very depressed economy. My stepfather had a decent job, which was rare, but there was a lot of poverty. I knew that I wanted more from life than the struggles I saw people go through just to survive. Although I didn't know exactly what I wanted, daydreaming was a pastime for me. The more I visualized what I wanted in life, the more defined my dreams became. Most of what I imagined was born from reading books, watching television and movies and choosing the things I wanted in my own life. I would spend hours in bed every night imagining my future down to the smallest detail. It is clear today that the things I visualized as a child I have manifested in my life as an adult.

I was born with an incredible focus and with it I have spent countless hours designing my life. Little did I know at a young age that what I was doing with all my daydreaming was manifesting or calling upon the law of attraction. My imaginings were always extremely detailed. I would drive around neighborhoods and look at all the houses and imagine myself buying the one I loved the most. I would visualize going shopping to pick out all the things I wanted to furnish it with and then perseverate for hours on the colors and the way the furniture was going to be laid out. I would get as detailed as the soap I would have on the counter in the bathroom and every plant that I would grow in the garden. Each night I would lie in bed, sometimes for hours, decorating, rearranging furniture, gardening, cooking, shopping, traveling and working. What I eventually discovered from watching my dreams come true was that I needed to be bold. I realized that I was keeping a limit on them in an attempt to be realistic and a reminder from childhood that I couldn't have it all. I never imagined what I couldn't realistically afford, like a sprawling Spanish hacienda; I imagined a house I could afford and what I would do to make it as close to my dream as possible. Even limiting my dreams by basing them in reality, I was able to manifest most everything I imagined and more. I eventually purchased my first house, but because I had a limited vision when I manifested it, I worked tirelessly to convert it into my dream home by upgrading, remodeling and adding on over the years until one day it was obvious that it would never be my dream home. I decided that I would begin all my daydreaming being financially independent so I didn't have anything holding me back from visualizing big. I began putting exactly what I wanted out there, but it didn't come. Imagine that. I spent three years dreaming of my perfect home. It was on a hill with incredible views. It was an adobe brick style hacienda with sprawling gardens and a red tile roof. I spent hours online looking at properties and everything I wanted was millions of dollars. Yet at night I would imagine it, what it looked like, what the views would be like, what I would be doing while I lived there. I imagined a garden, fruit trees, cooking, painting and even writing a book there. It would be my sanctuary. One day I looked online and saw an old adobe brick house on a hill with photos of seemingly beautiful views and, it was in our price range. I could tell by the photos that it needed a lot of work, but I convinced my partner to have a look. We met up with an agent at the house and it was crawling with people. There was something magic about it. I felt it the moment I stepped in the door. So did my partner. We experienced good vibrations and the scent of vanilla in the air like someone was baking cookies. There were views from every window, privacy, gardens, a fruit orchard and a wrap-around driveway with gates on both ends. It was bank owned and underpriced for even the depressed market of the time. We made an offer within 20 minutes of seeing it and it was accepted that night. Although the property was neglected for many years and needed a lot of work, I had a vision for it mapped out in my head as I walked through it. It was everything I dreamed of, but needed some TLC to bring it back to life. We now had to sell our current house in order to buy this one and so we hired an agent, prepped it, took pictures and put it on the market. We sold it in less than 24 hours for asking price. The seemingly flawless ease at which everything happened confirmed to me that it was right. Today I live in this house of my dreams. It's exactly as I always imagined it to be. I AM happy and grateful. All the pieces had to come into place yet, I had already manifested them as well: a loving relationship, a wonderful career and a passion for dreaming.

I always thought I would create my dream life with the success of my music, but instead I achieved it by following a different path. I always thought that I would be with my first partner for the rest of my life, yet it took a few tries to find my soul mate of 21 years. I dreamed I would live in a different place, but have manifested everything I want in another. Be present enough to recognize you may have already manifested every dream you have imagined, it's just wearing different clothes.

"Find the spark in your soul that is connected to everyone and run a current of unconditional love."

The common connection between all of us is God. The oneness that we share is woven by a chain of light through every soul and ties us together in a stream of consciousness. At times it is hard for me to understand why there are so many dark sinister people in the world when we are all God. There are those whom deliberately find ways to hurt people and feel pleasure from pain. Some people lie and manipulate the truth. They set people up and then sue them for monetary gain. There are those who feign injury or illness to collect workman's compensation and disability so they don't have to work. With so much dishonesty, it becomes hard to see their light. But if I look below the surface and into the core of their suffering, it begins to make better sense. Many people know no other way. They have been hurt so badly that they use their anger for protection. They try to pull people down so they don't have to be alone in their pain. They will do and say anything to focus attention outside of them. Any shred of decency or goodness that is offered to them is corrupted to fit the paradigm in which they live. It can be challenging for me to accept that they are one with me but they are.

The most important thing I have learned from darkness is to acknowledge that it exists without letting it draw me in and own any part of me. It is imperative I observe without attachment, listen without judgment and flow around it without touching it. I keep my focus on the truth that we share a connecting light source. I remember there is only one thing that can counter darkness, unconditional love. There must be forgiveness and detachment. My role is to love everyone unconditionally even if from a distance until they can do it for themselves. And if they can't, I send unconditional love anyway. I acknowledge the darkness then move away from it. I know that it needs to be there. It is perfect in its existence. I don't try to change it for it is part of the equation and the balance.

No matter who the person is, remember that you share a common spark of light. Find it and send a current of unconditional love through it. This spark is the one thing that binds both dark and light, good, bad and all of us together with the one undeniable thing that exists in every soul throughout eternity, unconditional love.

"Bring forth nothing less than what remains your greatest triumph."

The defining moment for me spiritually was when I completely understood the energy I had been able to see my whole life. The world of particles, space, planets, stars, humans, aliens, angels, demons, God and everything in between living together in a matrix of interconnected light called the multiverse. If at any time I ever begin to doubt this, another synchronicity comes to provide confirmation.

Three years after graduating from college, I accepted my first job as a recreation therapist at a locked psychiatric facility. I created and ran the psychosocial programing for 99 patients who were all ordered by the court system to be there. They were admitted with diagnosis ranging from paranoid schizophrenia to bi-polar disorder. While working there, I had a dream one night that I remembered in vivid detail. It was nighttime and I was standing in front of my mother's house in Big Pine. I walked up the stairs to the porch and entered the front door. It worried me that the door was unlocked. Once inside I began walking down the hallway that led to the bedrooms. At the end of the hall I could see the door to my parents' room open and my mom in bed sleeping. As I walked toward her room, I looked in through an open door to one of the bedrooms. There I saw my stepfather lying in bed with two female patients from the facility I worked at. I was instantly overcome with emotion and angered by the thought that he was cheating on my mother. I stood in the doorway in disbelief and observed that he wasn't having sex with them rather he was watching while they were having sex with each other. I tried to run into my mother's room to wake her and tell her what was going on, but I struggled in slow motion and couldn't get to her. I woke up yelling. The dream was absolutely bizarre. I put it out of my head and went back to sleep. The very next day I was at work leading a group of patients on how to recognize the signs and symptoms of a psychotic break. One woman that was in my dream was in attendance. For some reason, she was restless and having increased delusions. She kept asking me to call the nurse because she thought she was having a heart attack. This was one of her fixed delusions. She was in her early forties and physically healthy. As I tried to re-direct her, she became agitated. She stood up, pounded her book on the table, looked directly in my eyes and said, "Hey, by the way, I AM not a lesbian!" Immediately my hair stood on end as I tried to wrap my head around it. All day long it was on my mind. How in the world could she have known about my dream? It was then and there I knew that there was more to schizophrenia than a mental illness. She was able to see into my thoughts and read the energy stamp of the dream I had. I never looked at the disease the same way again. I believe that many schizophrenic minds are gifted with seeing and reading things most are unable to see. Why should I be surprised? After all, I was able to do the same thing.

It was also during this period I worked with a Catholic Director of Nurses who believed one of our young female residents suffered from demonic possession. In the hospital we worked at, when a code green was announced over the public address system it meant a "psychotic break" was taking place and all available staff was needed immediately. One day responding to a code I came upon a patient I knew well. She was sitting in a chair curled up in a ball rocking back and forth, yelling at the top of her lungs. This woman hadn't spoken a word for years. In fact in the five years I had worked there, I had never heard her speak a single one. She would often whistle like a bird and smile. She kept a marked-up bible at her bedside along with dozens of notebooks in which she had meticulously re-written the bible in her own words. In her bible she had crossed out each passage as she rewrote it in her notebooks. The psychiatrist said she suffered from hyper religiosity. There she sat in a chair curled up in a fetal position and had urinated on herself. She was speaking in tongues and jerking her head back and forth. It sounded as though she was actually speaking backwards. Suddenly she stopped and started speaking in a little girl's voice. Chills ran down my spine and every hair on my body stood on end. She told us she was scared and that the devil was coming to get her because she had been bad. After a couple of minutes of being fearful, she started speaking in what sounded like Latin, her eyes rolled into the back of her head and you could only see the whites of them. The social worker calmly asked, "Are you okay?" and she answered in a deep gravely voice, "I would never hurt her." "Who is speaking?" she asked. "I AM Satan". The patient continued to answer questions speaking in this tone until she started to convulse so violently that the nurses had to hold her down in the chair. She stopped shaking abruptly, opened her eyes and in a benevolent voice said, "Hello my children, I love all of you." When asked who she was, she responded, "I AM Jesus." This was either my first experience with a multiple personality disorder or a demonically possessed person. It was later that night and after several shots of Thorazine that she was assigned to one-on-one care in her room. She lay sleeping restfully. Hanging on the wall behind her bed was a crucifix that had been there for many years. Sometime after 10pm the mental health worker came screaming out of the room after she said the crucifix had flown off the wall as if some force knocked it across the room. She refused to go back in.

I have learned to accept that there is more to reality than what I once believed. I always keep an open mind. There are synchronicities every day that come to remind me. I don't ignore them.

"The raising of consciousness through love is the interconnected mission that we all share."

I believe we are programmed to elevate our consciousness and we experience opportunities to do so. And while we progress individually and our paths are vastly different, we share a common desire to love and be loved in return. I don't think there is a single person who doesn't have this programming in their DNA. Although some may chose to ignore or fight it, it is as fundamental as the need to eat, drink and sleep. We can deprive ourselves of all of these things, but eventually we will start to break down.

All too often, through a series of failed attempts, people begin to isolate and pull away from the hope that they will ever find someone to love and share their life with. I've heard it said, "I'm better off alone. I prefer it this way", yet I believe this couldn't be further from the truth. Loneliness comes when the human soul detaches from love, not lust, infatuation or desire. One cannot truly love another until they learn to love themselves. Until this is achieved, love remains one sided and often elusive.

On this tiny blue planet, we are but trillions of cells formed together with a soul that carries the entire collective unconscious of our world. Love itself teaches us the most valuable lessons in this life. Almost everything we learn revolves around it for at the heart of every issue is forgiveness and unconditional love. Yet throughout recorded history, there have been unthinkable horrors humans have inflicted upon each other. You would think that souls that have come here to elevate their consciousness and seek unconditional love wouldn't have it in them. I think of suicide bombers, 9/11, the Boston Marathon bombings or the co-pilot of German Wings flight 4U 9525 who murdered 150 innocent people. Hitler and other monsters in our history are forever in our collective memories. What causes people to do such unspeakable horrors? What if they were not human at all? I believe there are demons, entities, other worldly beings or whatever you want to call them, that pose as humans and wreak havoc for the sole purpose of derailing us. If a heart is purely dark then surely it's not human. While we are here to elevate our consciousness and discover the God we are, there are entities that will try and keep us from doing so. Have you ever seen someone completely spiral into depression, darkness or self-destruction through intoxication and addiction? It's likely they have called upon darkness. These trials will either destroy us, or eventually lead us to seek spiritual enlightenment. Darkness serves its purpose. Those who seek the answers eventually see it for what it is.

I believe there are reasons why it takes so long to understand our creation and existence here on earth. We are living in a constant illusion trapped by our senses. Biological life forms with evolving souls that reincarnate countless lifetimes until we can shatter the illusion. Our souls are eternal. Each life we learn something new and are reborn with a greater understanding and one step closer to the inter-dimensional spiritual realm from which we came. I know many people who claim there is no God. In contrast, I have spent hours talking with a man who expresses knowledge of creator level consciousness and details around the multiple laws and patterns that govern the multiverse. He has instant recollection of countless lives over millions of years through multiple cycles on different planets, in different dimensions and galaxies. He has a total understanding of everything. He has opened my mind to things I never could have imagined. The more I learn, the more I see that the laws governing this life are not simple. While they are complex, the easiest explanation to understand is that we are here to raise our consciousness through the act of giving and receiving unconditional love. In time, I believe we will all know everything there is to know and that somewhere locked in our DNA we already do.

"Everything is already perfect."

Almost every weekend I find myself thinking about things I think I need or feel I should do. It could be that the living room needs new furniture because I feel it is getting worn out, or my mattress needs replacing because it's sagging on one side. I notice that the paint in the hallway is dirty from the dog wiping his muzzle on it and needs to be cleaned up and the yard needs to be weeded. I think about the next car I want and start doing research. I go about my day from one thing to the next filling up the time with errands, shopping and surfing the web. I often get so wrapped up in the day that I forget to meditate or take the time to center myself. When this happens, it is easy to lose clarity and I often fail to see what is right in front of me, perfection. Everything I have is enough and I AM grateful for it. I just need to remind myself daily. Meditation allows me to slow down my mind so I can feel it. Reminding myself that everything is perfect keeps me focused on the positive. I have spent a good amount of time in this life perseverating on what I need instead of being grateful for what is right in front of me. Being grateful has evolved from a thought to a practice. I remind myself that there is always someone who is truly suffering more than I and yet, there is always a reason for everything. I make a choice to be happy. I reinforce this by repeating I AM happy, I AM healthy, I AM grateful throughout the day. It doesn't take long to find many things I AM grateful for and I concentrate on them. I believe that when I do this, I attract more of it to me. I have learned to slow down my mind, talk to myself, make amends for beating myself up, embrace and love myself. If I'm ever feeling stuck, all I have to do is look around, there is always something beautiful. As I AM writing this I can see the sky glowing orange from the sunset. I AM grateful for its beauty. Gratitude started small and grew bigger. In time it became easier to look for the positive things in life rather than dwell on the negative. For many years of my life I was conditioned to concentrate on the negative. I focused daily on the bad news around me and let it become interwoven into my consciousness and part of who I was and what I attracted. Until I realized and acknowledged this, I was stuck and attracting the wrong things. I found that the path to finding happiness was reflection and gratitude. Not only in things that were in front of me like a beautiful sunset, but also the meaning and gifts in everything that happens. It is an intricate world of balance and this simple reflection became an essential habit along the way.

"Trust your Intuition every time."

I had gone over a year without being sick. While everyone was catching colds or the flu that was going around, I remained untouched. I likened it to sleeping well, staying hydrated and eating healthy. Each morning I meditated and affirmed that I AM in perfect health and surrounded myself with loving and healing light. One day I ran into someone I had an estranged relationship with. While I always had great respect for them, I knew they harbored resentment for me. I could see them walking toward me and my intuition told me to turn the other way. At the time I was not sure why I felt that way, but I did not trust it and walked toward them even though I could have easily avoided it. When we met, we awkwardly hugged. We separated and I looked at them and asked, "How are you doing?" They responded, "I AM so sick" and coughed in my face. Three days later I found myself flat in bed with a fever barely able to move. This lasted for days and turned into an infection which required antibiotics that completely destroyed my stomach and caused me further distress. Just as I was getting over the sinus infection, I got sick from something I ate and three weeks later I had a fever and was achy again. I struggled so hard to recover that I ignored the lesson it was trying to teach me, "Gary, stop ignoring your intuition!" Once I got it, I recovered quickly. Even if you are like a moth to the flame, turn the other way when your intuition is telling you something. Be in the moment and think before acting. How many things can we avoid in life by pausing a moment to think before acting and trusting our intuition? Trust it and never look back. I manifested this encounter and this illness so I could learn to trust my intuition. Not only did I not trust it, I called this person to me to receive the lesson. I had recently been thinking about them in a less than loving light. This illness also came to show me the unhealthy connection I had and that I needed to love and forgive them. There are valuable lessons everywhere if I AM awake. Dr. Wayne Dryer said, *"If prayer is you talking to God, then intuition is God talking to you."*

"The most marvelous journey is on its way."

I can't always tell you why, but at times I feel that something amazing is about to happen. I just know it. It's like thinking you are going to win the lottery as you watch the first three numbers come up and you have all of them. It's that feeling of oh my God, something is happening here. It's an adrenaline rush. I get this feeling many times after meditating. In the aftermath of traveling through space and time while basking in the afterglow of divine connection with Source, I feel it. The most marvelous journey is on its way!

If you look back at your life, I AM certain you will find it has been an incredible journey. If there is one thing that I hope to do by sharing mine, it is to inspire you to retrace the footsteps of your own life and to contemplate the many lessons and paths that have lead you to today. Each and every one of us has a unique experience of life and if you retrace your footsteps, you may be surprised to find how synchronicities, grace and perhaps even miracles have appeared along the way. I found that the key to sculpting my future was to understand my past and what the key lessons along the way have taught me. I had to be fearless and remember all of it in detail no matter how painful it became. Through this process I learned that no matter how tough or how horrible I thought the lesson was, there was something good that came from it. While there were times I was unable to see it right away, by taking the time to deeply examine and meditate on it, it became clearer why every single thing happened the way it did and I was eventually able to see the good that came from it.

When the cosmic delusion was revealed as sensory seduction and illusion, everything I could see, hear, taste, smell and touch grew boring and I had no choice but to start this journey of spiritual enlightenment. I decided that it wasn't enough to live with my eyes closed so I opened them to the unknown and began to explore. I knew from birth there was much to learn here. I remember vividly at one month old as my mother laid me under the Christmas tree, eyes wide open, mesmerized by the twinkling lights, thinking, I'm back; I'm in a body again, I can see and feel things again. I was excited because I knew I was just about to start an amazing journey.

"We are all one gigantic soul of interconnected light."

I believe that if you are on this planet, you are connected to everyone and every thing here and we are all one gigantic connected light. Each of us has a life force and soul at the command center of our creation. I AM here to live, learn and advance my soul to a higher spiritual understanding of existence. Of all life forms on this planet, being human makes it hard as we are seduced and clouded by our senses. Wayne Dyer always said, "We are spiritual beings having a human experience." I also believe I've known the people in my life before from other incarnations, different relationships and places. We are souls that travel as a family and come together life after life to interact and live out our karma. We are continually presented with lessons to teach us how to elevate our consciousness and ultimately our souls. Every single person I have loved, thought I hated, admired, despised, embraced and shunned has been here to teach me one thing: that I AM capable of unconditional love. Today I no longer have the capacity to hate anyone. This is an evolution. Ultimately, I believe if you can say you have mastered this life and move unaffected through its existence in a fluid state of unconditional love, then it is likely you will not reincarnate here again. Each of us knows at some point in our evolution whether or not we still need to be here on earth. I used to think I was ready to move on, but now realize there is much left to learn. Our souls upon being reincarnated, with rare exceptions, have the previous lives erased from our memory. But have we truly forgotten everything we have ever experienced from other lives?

Have you ever felt an unexplainable connection to some place, someone or something? Perhaps you watched a television show on ancient Rome and you felt your heart ache with longing. You know that you must go there before you die. Maybe you read an article about ancient Egypt and the pyramids and can't stop thinking about it. You long to see them in person and explore a pharaoh's tomb. You find yourself collecting documentaries on Egypt and have a painting of the river Nile hanging on your living room wall. You love the piano, you have always wanted to play and you picture yourself playing a concert in front of thousands and bask in the adoration of a standing ovation. You somehow find that you are a natural at playing and don't even need to read music, you play by ear. You meet someone and hit it off right away, it's as if you have known each other your whole life. You find yourself talking for hours and hours and discover you have lived parallel lives. You meet their family and they accept you as one of their own. Everyone feels as if you've always been a part of the family. Have you ever ended up somewhere in your life entirely by mistake or chance and have it turn out to be the best thing that has ever happened to you? These events are synchronicities. They are unexplainable and magical at the same time. I think we all have had similar experiences. I believe these are glimpses of past lives and remembering who we once were.

I remember shortly after finishing school I was looking for my first position in healthcare. My friend Kevin who had been working in the field for over a decade told me about a position with a small not-for-profit organization with a small nursing home right on the beach. He told me that it would be the best place to get my feet wet. He said I needed to speak to a gentleman named Vito who he said he didn't have the contact for, but to look in the Sunday paper and I would see the ad. He mentioned it said: small 45-bed not-for-profit nursing home on the beach seeking a mission driven administrator to oversee operations. I looked in the paper and there was only one ad for administrator and it read exactly as Kevin stated; however, the contact was Wendy. I called the number and was scheduled right away for an interview. A couple of weeks later I was offered the position. I loved the job right away and felt like it was home. It was a wonderful mission-driven organization that aligned completely with my values. It was a year later, I was at a convention with Kevin and he introduced me to Vito. It wasn't until then that I learned there was another nursing home down the street looking for an administrator at the same time. Vito had taken the ad down that weekend and I ended up interviewing with Wendy instead. It was synchronicity that brought me to my job and fate would have it that a year later Vito's nursing home closed and I would have been out of a job. Seventeen years later I AM still with the same organization.

One day I had left work early due to a sore lower back. I decided I would go home, take some ibuprofen and try to sleep it off. As I approached my car in the parking garage, I noticed that it was filthy and badly needed a wash. As I drove up the hill leaving La Jolla, there on my left was the Pearl Car Wash beckoning me. I pulled in, paid for my carwash and went outside to sit and wait. As I exited the door I noticed that just outside was a woman offering chair massages. She knowingly looked at me and smiled, "Would you like a massage while you wait." "Would I!" I straddled the chair and she began to massage my sore back, neck and shoulders pointing out that I was tight and my muscles were having spasms. I told her, "What I really need is a chiropractor." She said that it was perfect timing because she worked for one and he could see me right away. She got on her mobile phone, called the office and set up an appointment. I got in my clean car and drove down the road to the office. When I got inside, there were many people waiting. I sat down and picked up a book of testimonials. At the front of the book was a bio on how Dr. Klein received the calling to become a Chiropractor. Something felt strangely familiar and as 45 minutes wore on I became frustrated and wanted to leave. Just as I was ready to stand up and go, my pain said, "stay" and they called my name. I went into an office were a young woman tried to sell me a package of visits, I declined and once again wanted to leave, yet something made me stay. I was guided to an exam room and shortly after, Dr. Klein came in the room and introduced himself. He kept looking at me intensely, walking from side to side examining me like a piece of art. He furrowed his brow and said, "Where are you from?" an odd question to be asked. I told him I was from Burbank and he continued to walk side-to-side looking at me, "Where did you go to elementary school?"

"Bret Hart". "Who was your kindergarten teacher?" "Mrs. Onstadt." "Really! She was mine too!" he exclaimed. He proceeded to go through a list of names asking if I knew any of them. Finally he asked, "Do you know Jenny Trax?" "Yes! Her brother Danny and I were born in the same hospital by the same doctor on the same day and her mom and mine are good friends, we grew up together!" It turns out that his mother was my tutor in elementary school when I was only five-years-old. I used to go to his house every week. We both called our mothers on our cell phones and they spoke for the first time in decades. What a small world? How in the world did this man nearly 37 years later recognize me? I didn't look even remotely the same as I did when I was five and he was only four. When I queried, he could only say, "I just knew that I knew you." Souls travel in families.

"It's not about me, it's about respecting them."

Have you ever had a situation where someone has turned a fun night out into something very uncomfortable? How did you handle it?

I think of a time when I was out to dinner with friends and a boisterous man at the bar was screaming so loudly at the basketball game on the television that everyone in the restaurant was interrupted from their dinner conversation. Nobody said anything because they were feeling him project, "Mess with me and there is going to be a fight."

For many, dinner was unpleasant. For me, I remembered that I AM the creator of my own experience. I could have said something and created a scene, said nothing and let it ruin my evening, accept that it is the basketball finals and let him yell away, ask to be moved to another room or ask for a box and finish my meal at home. Each of these actions would produce different results. I believe this man felt the energy projected at him and in his drunken state it only served to taunt him more. He was attracting exactly what he wanted and feeding off of it. I chose to laugh and accept that he was drunk, having a good time and I enjoyed my dinner.

Another night I went to my favorite sushi restaurant and just as my meal arrived the child at the table across from me started to throw a tantrum, crying, wailing and disrupting everyone in the restaurant. People were looking around, staring at the young mother trying to console her upset child to no avail. I could hear people saying, "Why doesn't she just take the kid outside, what is wrong with people?"

One of the most important lessons I have learned in my life is that I create my own experiences. I can choose to let experiences upset me or realize I AM in control of the situation. If I don't feel up to dealing with drunken people, then I don't go to a bar. If I don't want to hear screaming children, I don't go out to a family style restaurant. If for whatever reason, I don't want to deal with crowds, I don't go out.

We live in a world of many people and personalities. Each with varied backgrounds, cultures and upbringings. I can't expect everyone to behave the way I think they should. I AM the creator of my experience with every move I make. I can choose to accept that a crying baby is beautiful or annoying. I remember, they are just arriving here and trying to make sense of all the craziness going on around them, their behavior isn't about me. I can chose to see the drunken sports fan having a great time and be happy that they are. I can turn a bad situation around by changing the way I think or making a choice to do something different and I remember it's not about me and more about respecting them.

"It is not what we have or will get, it is only unconditional love that matters."

I can have whatever I want. But often I have failed to see that what I have asked for is usually right in front of me.

I have known loveless relationships. Sometimes it was love giving way to routine and the passion dies. It may have been the person I desired physically, yet they didn't meet my emotional needs or vice versa. Whatever it was, there was something unfulfilling about it. Many times it was something that had absolutely nothing to do with them and everything to do with me. Maybe they didn't touch me, or kiss me or look at me the way I wanted or they did and I just seemed to be annoyed by it. Usually I would arrive at the truth after careful exploration of why I created it.

I know a woman who has been in a relationship for years with a man that will not touch her intimately during sex. She has tried everything she can to win his desire to no avail. She is beautiful, works out daily, in amazing physical shape and still nothing. She doesn't understand that this has nothing to do with her. She is resentful yet stays with him because she feels he physically represents the man of her dreams. He is the beautiful specimen that she visualized her whole life except that when creating him, she left out the fine details such as being emotionally intelligent, intimate and strongly attracted to her. She got exactly what she asked for. There is another man in her life. One who is a good friend and absolutely worships and adores her. He would touch and love her like no other man, but she has no physical attraction to him. She is unwilling to even think about being with him because then she would be settling for less than her perfect physical match. I have explored with her that the more you love unconditionally, the more you discover that a person's looks are a lower priority on the scale when finding a life partner and their ability to love unconditionally the highest. We have all walked away from soul mates one time or another because we were being clouded by our senses. Remember to explore your feelings, "There is something about them" and open your heart to lead the way. Overlook the shell to find the pearl.

"Surround every soul with love and light for they are you."

One of the things I enjoy most about going to parties is meeting new people. After a few cocktails people start to loosen up and have fun. The more drinks, the more people open up, about everything. It is then I start to hear their stories. Everyone has something they want to share and it is here in these conversations that we often reconnect, find a soul mate, a friend, a teacher and even a Master walking amongst us. Magic are the moments I meet new people. It is such a gift when our souls connect and reconnect. I try to surround each person I meet with love and light for they are one with me.

I have often wondered how people become isolated into groups, bigoted, and intolerant of anyone different from them. We learn about life from those around us. Depending on our life's circumstances, this may have excluded us from having friends with anyone other than our own race, sexual orientation, religion, background or lifestyle. Many people like to stay in their comfort zone, but they may be forced to venture a little outside of it at work and parties. I met a woman at a party who discovered during our conversation that I was gay. She couldn't stop shaking her head at how I just didn't look or act that way. She went on to share that she didn't have any gay friends in her circle and had limited exposure. She couldn't understand why some gay men were effeminate and acted like girls. That really seemed to bother her. I listened openly and could clearly see that somewhere in her upbringing and within her circle of friends there was gay bashing and homophobia around effeminate men. This couldn't have possibly bothered her unless someone taught her that it should. When she asked for my opinion on why some gay men were effeminate and I was not, I gave an honest answer. I told her that I grew up in a world where being effeminate would have attracted bullying, harassment and violence. I didn't share my personal experiences, but I explained to her that men of my generation had to assimilate and behave according to social norms or be subjected to abuse. I told her we live in a different world today where people are able to be themselves and so you find more people being comfortable in their skin. I told her that I look past all of it to the soul inside and love people for who they are. I told her that everybody bleeds the same and we all have the same capacity to feel. We are all one, even the effeminate gay men. Why not just love them for who they are? She thought about it and shook her head, "I hear you." I know she did. She asked me if I had grown up today, would I act effeminate and I again answered honestly, "I don't know." I believe we are all products of our life's experiences and upbringing. We learn how to act and behave based on the positive or negative reinforcement we get. Some of the most bigoted people in the world were never given the chance to know better. It is those who were given the chance to know better that suffer the most. Hate, ignorance and fear attract the same so does unconditional love and you get to choose what you want. If you look hard enough, you will find yourself in everyone.

"If you look you'll see love is right in front of you."

I believe that when many of us are around crowds of people whether it is out with friends at parties or other social situations, we pull into a world of self-consciousness. Introvert or extrovert, conscious or unconscious, we decide whether or not to introduce ourselves to others, possibly start a conversation and begin the dance of finding common ground. Sometimes we don't engage because we are uncomfortable with how we look, feel or fit it. Other times we become our ego. I may meet someone and the conversation becomes all about the ego. What do you do for a living? Where do you live? It may be that someone is really interested or it's a springboard for expressing who they are, where they've been and what they've seen. Sometimes the conversation sounds like, "Me, me, me and I, I, I". I have often found myself alone in a room full of people.

Over time, I have learned to become a witness. I consciously stop, look at the person in front of me and make a decision to find out who they are and forget about myself or making my point. I find that if I take the time to get to know someone without interjecting anything at all to the conversation other than questions, acknowledgement and understanding I see something remarkable happen. I witness the unfolding of their past and glimpses into their future. I see their ups and downs and lessons of their current incarnation. The most striking thing, the undercurrent of all existence begins to emerge, the quest and desire to love and be loved. It is the God in all of us, the one commonality we share. Not a single soul on this planet is programmed differently and so it is certainly the one thing we can all come together on. Those who are teachers and those who are followers emerge. One who can consciously give unconditional love and support to everyone is a teacher. Unconditional love is the one thing we are all here to learn. No matter who you are talking with, if you look and listen deeply enough, love is sitting right in front of you. Find that love and nurture it, become the Source from which it came. It is here that we can become mindful and look past the material and into the spiritual.

"Each soul that comes here must discover they are God."

I grew up knowing that there was another world operating unseen to our conscious mind. A spiritual realm filled with divine creatures and ancient wisdom. I was influenced by a Christian upbringing. I learned of a powerful judging God that had complete domain over all existence on this planet. God was a father figure who sat in a throne in the sky somewhere in heaven where a perfect joyful life for all his followers existed. Nobody was ill, all your favorite animals went there and deceased family and friends who believed in Jesus, his son, lived there in one of the many mansions created for them by the nature of accepting said son as their personal savior. Everything about God was outside of me. It was His creation, His animals, His planet, His people and His son. He judged and He expected adherence to His laws and commandments. If bad things happened, surely it was because I had done something to earn His wrath. His people cried, "How could you let my son die, how could you allow this horrible murder, this rape, this war, this starvation, this existence? What kind of God would allow such things?" The answer from the pulpit was always, "God works in mysterious ways and we put our faith in Him."

All the beliefs on this planet both ancient and forward require an element of so called blind faith or at least adherence to some religion's doctrine. We are told not to question or doubt for God is powerful and His wrath and vengeance fierce. Fear is used to scare the deviant into submission and assimilation. Nearly everyone who is born on this planet is subjected to one form of religion or another and commanded or forced to assimilate said beliefs in their day-to-day existence without question. Most souls are at one time or another in their life force fed another man's experience of God. We are often brainwashed from childhood and to deviate or move away from said beliefs comes with punishment, often the loss of family and friends and their love and the threat of hell.

I have come to find peace in knowing that God isn't outside of us. I AM God. You are God. We are God. We are the most powerful creators in the universe. We create our own existence with every move we take. You see, the cries of His people can all be answered. God does allow horrible things to happen because humankind is God. We are all God and most human suffering comes at the hand of humankind and the result of misused God-given power. It is the absence of God self-realization in all of us that creates struggle in the world. We may all at one time or another misuse our God-given power by not knowing the power we wield in our own thoughts, hands and hearts. Men waging wars in the name of God are simply waging it on themselves not realizing that they are Gods yet to realize that unconditional love is the only real truce. You are God and the purpose of life is giving and receiving unconditional love. All life's experiences revolve around getting us to this one place. We are one interconnected string of lights pulsating at different frequencies all yearning for the same love from one another. Seek the God in yourself and there you will find the truth.

What of the father who becomes a terrorist as the children he loves sit at home with their mother while he is out indiscriminately killing innocent people in the name of God? Is he God? I believe he is. Maybe lost, blinded and indoctrinated into hate, another soul waiting to learn the truth. Do you think this man doesn't love his wife or children? I believe he does. Do you think that he doesn't have the same capacity for unconditional love as you? I do. It may be as simple as he was never given the chance to know any other way. Or what if he is one of many non-human entities (or call them demons) brought here to create horror for billions of souls whether to fulfill karmic law and or to bring about elevation of consciousness? I understand this is a heavy and controversial statement. But I truly believe that when we realize that we are God, we begin to see the control that we have and that everything exists perfectly within the laws of this creation.

"Seek God first and all things will come to you for you are God."

Through karma I have come to learn many lessons, each one building on the others until a harmony like none I have ever known lives with me each day. If I were forthcoming about my understanding of this planet, the laws of this creation and our creator, I would likely alienate 90% of the readers as the truth is not simple, the destination is and so this is what I've tried to concentrate on. While there are many planes of existence each with their own laws, we all share the same destination, oneness with Source and unconditional love. I believe there is no other end for anyone in this infinite existence and multiverse.

There are multiple laws that govern our existence on earth. I have heard many proclaim that the law of attraction doesn't exist. That it is made up, new age, hocus-pocus. Those who profess this may ask, "Where is my billion dollars? My mansion? Where's my perfect life?" Often it is ego that asks. We must all look at our part in this creation. I believe the law of attraction is only one law; there is karma and other laws at work. When dynamic volition doesn't produce the desired results, there is a good reason. If you think about it long enough, you will understand why. We don't always get everything the way we want it and for a reason. In each of us there is a sacred genetic code that science is only now beginning to unravel and understand. In this divine code, given to us by our creator, lies the answers to everything. Those answers are all inside you if only you shut down the senses long enough to connect and activate their signal. Some people have a mutation in their DNA that allows them to have glimpses into the vast unknown almost naturally, think Einstein. Others struggle and some never even think about it. For most, the only way to activate this ancient DNA is through meditation. When we meditate, we tap into the vast God consciousness that connects us all together and to our own God self. Think of the synapses in our brains being slowed down by alcohol, we tell our hand to pick up something and it can't, we are intoxicated. The only way for the signal to get through again is when the alcohol dissipates and leaves our body unblocking the neural pathways. Same with the God receptors in our brain, the only way for God to come through is if we unblock the receptors by detaching ourselves from our senses during meditation. Each time we meditate, it dissolves the blockage until the full God energy permeates our consciousness. Meditation is like learning a new language. You must learn techniques and practice them until it becomes natural. You must also do it every day. If we don't, the receptors begin to clog again the signals stop coming through. The inundation of everything hitting our senses creates a powerful God blocking substance that renders the soul deprived of the universal consciousness of I AM self-awareness.

"I forgive me, I love myself."

I have done many things in my life that can still make me cringe when I think about them. I feel badly for having ever hurt anyone. The lessons I have learned have been huge and for many years affected my self-esteem with negative self-talk and beating myself up around what I should have, could have done. This kept me from loving myself.

Negative self-talk presented as a conversation in my head that told me things like, "You're sick, you're stupid, you're cruel, you deserve this, you're ugly and you're fat." I used to spend hours cleaning, working out excessively and making sure that I and everything around me looked good because I believed that if everything looked good on the outside, then I was okay. But on the inside I wasn't, even though everyone thought I was so together. I was still a little boy that felt like he let his family and friends down and so I would beat myself up. Maybe not all the time, but in the background a self-deprecating tape was playing. It wasn't until I went to the Oprah weekend and she led us through the meditation that for the first time in my life, I was able to forgive myself. I was able to learn that I could look at myself in the mirror each day and say, it wasn't your fault, you are okay, you are worthy, be good to yourself, you're beautiful and I love you. I could take my hand, place in on my heart and rub back and forth and repeat, you are beautiful, I love you and I forgive you. I started doing this each day in my meditations and each day I grew stronger. My confidence grew and I found that my negative self-talk turned into positive self-affirmation and love. The first step to unconditional love is to forgive and love oneself. If we can't love ourselves, then we cannot love others. If we cannot love others, then we cannot tap into the universal God consciousness, which is, the I AM in all of us. Unconditional love starts with loving yourself.

"We are here for spiritual assimilation into unconditional love."

The interesting thing about love to me is how often it is cited as many different feelings. If you were to ask a hundred people what love is, you would get answers as varied as the people themselves. Many say love is sexual attraction, passion, desire, needing, wanting and self-sacrifice, and while I believe that these may be ingredients of love, they never resonated as the definition of it to me.

I believe that if you ask the question during meditation and spend enough time contemplating the meaning of love, it will come to you. As a creator, if you seek, the answers are programmed in your DNA and will reveal themselves in time. For me, unconditional love is the feeling I get when I detach from what I can see, hear, touch, smell and taste and tune into my sixth sense. It was when I understood why I incarnated and chose the mother and father I did, that tears fell down my face from the sheer gratitude I felt. It's when I had a crystal clear moment of understanding exactly why something happened in my life and the gift received from it. Again, tears flowed naturally down my face. It's when I think of someone and the thought brings tears of joy and gratitude to my eyes. It's tears in the moment I see someone I hold dearly in my heart and haven't seen for a long time. It's that thought or moment that pulls the air from my lungs and interrupts the flow of breath long enough for tears to flow.

Tears are a gift. Inside each tear is the most powerful ingredient known to humankind, love. Unconditional love is accepting that regardless of anything someone may have done to hurt me, I can look past it and feel the joy of their existence and relevance in my life. Unconditional love loves the people that hurt me and understands that they are part of me and I of them. Unconditional love recognizes that I AM one with everything and only love and enlightenment can stop the pain. By hating anything I only hate myself. I start the spark of unconditional love by loving myself, others and forgiving everyone and everything bad that has ever been in my life. I cannot experience enlightenment without forgiveness nor can I feel unconditional love. There are many ways I have felt and experienced love as a human. I began to better understand what love meant to me by exploring websites like Upworthy and Youtube searching the keyword "tissues needed". I explored what it is that will make almost any human who watches it cry and there I have found love. The connections and answers came to me like magic. Love is everything, everywhere and a life without it is one of the most painful existences on earth. Love is tears.

I believe a spiritual existence can only come from exploring the sixth sense. If I never slow down my mind and senses enough to experience this plane, I cannot experience true spiritual enlightenment and unconditional love in its purest form. To give unconditional love, I must be attuned to my sixth sense. Lifetimes of experience and careful meditation have opened the door. When I was ready, the teacher came, when I was open, the answers flowed, when the realization came, unconditional love was the only thing that mattered.

"Teach love for there is no greater power in this earth."

There was a demand that the universe placed on me in the moment of my enlightenment. That is to practice what I've learned each day and to share my experience with others. Not to proselytize, but to share without pushing my views on others. Sharing how it has affected me alone. How I came about my activation and examples of how it changed my life. If I don't talk about my experience, I will never fulfill my purpose to help if only one other person attain spiritual enlightenment and feel unconditional love. When the truth-seeking soul is ready, the teacher will come. I remember the beginning of my journey when I was first introduced to Paramahansa Yogananda. After being told by several people I had to read his Autobiography, I tried but couldn't. I'd fall asleep, lose interest and it sat on a shelf gathering dust. I was not yet ready to read his book and was not, until the time was right. When I finally did read it, it changed my life. This was the same for the *I AM Discourses* by St. Germain and Guy Ballard. I simply could not have read this book until I was ready to receive it. It was these books that opened me up to understanding my own inherent gifts and my sixth sense. I was for years a live wire and conduit for spiritual lightening without any structure to the intensity I was receiving it. If there is any corruption in this light structure, it is that these ancient tools given us have been marketed and packaged in get rich quick and have what you want schemes. In Matthew 6:33 Jesus said, "But seek ye first the kingdom of God, and his righteousness; and all these things shall be added unto you". We must own the God in ourselves and seek daily to be in this presence and only then will all else come to us. We cannot seek first to be rich because it is contrary to the spiritual law of abundance. One of the commandments states love your neighbor as yourself. We cannot love our neighbor if we don't love ourselves. Seek ye first the kingdom of God that is you, unconditional love and then teach this love for there is no power greater than this on earth.

"Seeking souls awaken, see the light and know it is ever expanding."

Humankind has been seeking enlightenment since the beginning of existence. It has come one person at a time and then large movements throughout history. I believe that when a soul awakens to realms of higher thinking, it opens itself to the programmed DNA of wisdom imparted by our creator. It is there that I began to understand the magnitude of the energetic laws of this creation and other laws that govern our existence on earth. I believe that earth is not the only realm where life exists. There are infinite planets, galaxies and dimensions that exist within the multiverse each with their own creator and laws. To be here on earth is to be confined to this set of rules for this creation. I also believe that life exists everywhere in the matrix of everything and rarely, if ever, do creations interact on a level visible to the human eye. All creation exists simultaneously without time restriction. Everything is happening at once everywhere. There is no time, it simply is. In humankind's journey in this creation, there is one constant that is always there that ties us infinitely to every other creation in the infinite multiverse and that is The Light. You only need to close your eyes and behold the scattered dots of vibrating white, blue and black particles enveloped within a sea of golden light. It is this energy that is everywhere at once in the infinite matrix.

Imagine darkness that goes on forever, nothing can be seen in this total blackness. The multiverse without programming is simply this space without creation. When a creator creates, galaxies, dimensions and life they are formed by programming their existence into the black space. Think of a blank computer screen being programmed with numbers and symbols to create a 3D image of man. Every creation is built into this space all at different frequencies, distances, dimensions and rules. A soul may live in any one these creations. As the laws of this creation are better understood, one can begin to travel across the matrix and experience them through the vehicle of meditation. As the sixth sense develops, it becomes easier to tap into the energy fields that allow this transcendent experience. A friend taught me a highly enlightened and channeled meditation. He told me to imagine two circular spheres, one rotating in a clockwise direction and the other rotating opposite. He told me to watch them spinning so quickly that they form a sphere. He said to tell the sphere to advance it's spinning to light speed then to increase the speed to ten times the speed of light, a hundred times, a thousand, a million, ten million, a trillion, a quadrillion and so on. Each step the sphere enlarges. He stated that once he got into 100 quadrillion times the speed of light, he began to see advanced alien cultures, near formless humanoid beings in spaceships flying thru hyperspace avoiding suns and looping around constellations in small light cruisers. As I did this meditation, I started with the speed of light and then shortly went to infinite speed of light. At this point I had the realization of I AM God infinite light speed in the universe, our sun is but a dot of light in the pure creation of unconditional love that is the foundation of the matrix. I AM that I AM. We are God, the most powerful creator in the universe and the Light that is ever expanding. We are all able to do this if willing to give it the time and practice.

"Give what you can and always be generous."

I have talked about giving to those less fortunate than us, but giving isn't always reserved for those without. Giving time to those struggling is equally important. Sometimes giving means doing absolutely nothing but listening. We are all here to help one another. Just listen and acknowledge those who need it. I often find people sharing with me the most intimate details of their lives. I never probe or ask questions, I just listen. This single act of kindness has the power to change an outcome or more, open someone up to healing. Often through self-exploration and conversation comes enlightenment. If you are ever seeking answers to questions, call upon your most trusted friends. The more people involved, the better the solution. Above this, it is equally important to take time in meditation to contemplate the situation, visualize how you want the outcome to be and listen to your inner voice.

When I was in Hawaii this past year I had the opportunity to listen to Wayne Dyer speak. He talked about giving, taking care of others and his uncontrollable desire to provide for people. It is natural when you are in a state of unconditional love to want to give. There are several people that he is helping and makes it a point to go to the bank each week to get money and make sure that an envelope is delivered to them. These acts of kindness unplug receptors in our brains and allow the pure flow of love to begin. The giving does not come from ego, but rather from our true nature as humans. It is our true nature to love and help each other. If you can't give financially to those in need, give from your heart and be generous.

"My light is everywhere."

I had the opportunity to attend a conference with fellow co-workers recently and was given an incredible insight into human nature. The entire scene unfolded in real time as I watched many top executives begin to partake in what I call the drunken social dance of one-upmanship. The evening started the same each time with cocktails. There was small talk mostly, how is your work, spouse, trips you've taken. When the second and third rounds came, the conversation loosened up and took on a flavor of who could be the loudest, funniest, and a jostling for the attention of others. The more the alcohol flowed, the more sarcastic the conversation became until many of the team were telling each other off and degrading each other to be funny. As I sat and watched with smile on my face, people would look at me, my half-finished cocktail, the second round sitting next to it and say,

"Gary, drink up." I smiled, sat and watched while others wanted desperately for me to be like them or to justify their behavior which each of them felt guilty about the next day. I continued to move conversations one on one to a more comfortable place for me. In doing this, one co-worker opened up to me about a text conversation her spouse was having with a co-worker that she felt uncomfortable and somewhat jealous about. She told me that she confronted her husband and that it caused a rift in their relationship. She felt defeated, sad, betrayed and insecure. I read the text and it was mildly flirtatious. I explained to her that by confronting him it would only serve to bring about the very thing she feared the most. The more you fear something the greater the chances you will draw it into your life. Sometimes the most important thing to remember is that we cannot control another person. Even if her husband wanted to cheat on her, there is nothing she could do about it. If she continued to confront him on something he was innocent of and based on her own fears, it would serve to build resentment, hiding and degradation of intimacy in their relationship. This could lead to the very thing she was afraid of. The focus should be on loving him, accepting him for who he is, not trying to change him. I told her to play out the tape in its entirety and if ultimately he wanted to leave her, she would be okay. The issue was about her, not him. She had to know inside that no matter what happened, she would be okay. When we love ourselves unconditionally, we never have to place our wellbeing or worth on the actions or opinions of others. She turned to me with the most loving eyes and said, "Thank you, you're right, I feel awful, I want to call him right now." The next day she sent me a message, "By the way, loved my time with you and your wonderful advice. It was such a blessing when we talked last night. Thank you!" So, in the midst of sarcastic, drunken chaos, I find the calm and seek out pain behind the actions and seek to help with love in my heart. There is nothing good about sarcasm and on some level, there is truth in it and ultimately it is hurtful. I feel that using humor to degrade another is the ultimate form of insecurity. It sits on the polar opposite of my nature. I didn't feel the need to fit in; I could serve as the one working quietly behind the scenes with love. Wherever you are, there is your light, how do you want it to shine?

"I AM unconditional love and I AM everywhere."

Wherever I go, there I AM. I take my energy stamp with me. This includes my strengths, weaknesses, insecurities and a lifetime of karmic lessons. My actions are the cumulative effect of this and may be opposite of my true self. It is not easy to be true to oneself especially in a world where we are conditioned to respond and behave in a certain socially accepted way. I AM a cosmic energy field constantly seeking out, reading my environment and ultimately protecting myself from invading unwanted energies. I move fluid through my environment and respond or take on the shape of where I AM at in any given moment. If I AM in a room full of partying people, chances are I will be too. If sitting in an airport lobby waiting to board a plane with others and the person in front of me keeps yawning, I will likely do the same and so will those around me. We are all connected in this unseen energy matrix. The overwhelming connection often keeps most of us from reaching out and making contact. The energy it takes to connect with everyone in a large room is enormous and so one will unconsciously shrink their energy to either themselves or the person in front of them. I do not have that ability, I connect to every soul in the room and often this can be overwhelming. I can walk in a room and sense the over-arching emotion present, feel the arguments someone just had or the resentment someone is feeling toward the person next to them. The more that I tune out, the more I move away from my true self. Next time you are in a room full of strangers, tune in, pay attention to the energy and connect your light to everyone. What begins to happen will astonish you. You will start to recognize people.

"I AM working in perfect unison with the universe, sending parallel waves of light and unconditional love to every existence."

While recognizing others within the realm of the collective unconscious, I focus my attention on the true constant that surrounds me, parallel waves of light that permeate each existence on this planet. When tuning into a room full of people this light travels through the air and connects every object in a sea of molecules and, more importantly, connects each soul to the other. The key to enlightenment is tuning into this in the moment. To ponder it, even believe it, is different than making it a part of your conscious awareness in the moment. The distractions I experience in my daily life often become the barrier to this awareness. Balancing out cognitive need for structure with the awareness of a room is a skill that takes practice. If no matter what is happening in the room I AM consciously sending out unconditional love to every receiver, I will receive this energy back. Unconditional love carries a frequency that is the highest most recognizable one on this planet. Walking around the room and hugging everyone, smiling and beaming is not necessary. Unconditional love in the form of feeling and thought carries an energy signature in the form of light emanated by the very electrical nature of every molecule created during the thought process. This wave of light, when projected, permeates every molecule with its signature. This one act can singularly change the energy of the room and mood of a group or outcome of a situation. Imagine if everyone were emanating these same waves how powerful the love in the room would be. It is similar to being in a room of people meditating together. Slow your thinking, tune into the collective unconscious, find your higher God self and become the I AM presence sending unconditional love out to the universe. When you have discovered your place of unconditional love, take that feeling and repeat, I AM

God, I AM unconditional love, I AM sending love to everyone. Make it the current of your existence.

"Like the light in a diamond, the entire universe lives within every cell of your existence. Within this light lives unconditional love, let it sparkle."

Have you ever seen a crystal hanging in the sunlight create rainbows all over a room? This is how unconditional love emanates from our minds, body and soul. Unconditional love is filtered through us directly from the Source and creates a signature as profoundly beautiful as a rainbow reflected on a wall. As we tune our instrument, unconditional love can be sent out into the universe infinitely like music through speakers. Every cell in our existence is as infinite as the universe we live in. We can travel out beyond our solar system into the mathematical theoretical multiverse of infinity and conversely do the same within each molecule of our body. We are all part of the infinite multiverse in every cell of our existence. The light allows us to travel without barrier and exist within the realm of timelessness. We are light. In meditation, I take unconditional love and explode it into the universe. Our minds are prisms and when the Light comes through us, we convert its waves into the laws of our existence and the rainbow of our purpose. Unconditional love is at one speed, the law of attraction another. Like white light travels through a prism at different speeds and makes a beautiful rainbow, Source energy travels though our chakras at different speeds to give us life and allow us to feel the amazing vibration of unconditional love. The rainbow is a symbol of beauty as is human life. Both created by the Light. These energies travel within the light and cannot be stopped once set in motion. This is why we must be mindful of our thoughts. Unconditional love sparkles like light through a diamond. Imagine sending this out to everyone and everything in our universe every day.

"The light is wherever there is light and there is always light."

People have used the terms light and dark energies since the beginning of recorded history. In understanding good versus evil, I have come to believe that things that are good are carried by light and things that are absent of light are the realms of evil. This comes from the idea that light comes from the Source, which is unconditional love, an energy that travels only on waves of light. When light is blocked and darkness ensues, we become evil and corrupt. There is not however, one existing without the other. There is a perfect balance in the universe and within the laws of our existence this is a constant. Even within the evil person, light exists yet clouded from the prism of his or her mind. Everyone has the ability to receive the light, yet often needs the darkness to live out the life experience he or she came to get, so the mind is clouded.

I speak frequently about God receptors being clogged. This is a simple way of saying that the light is being blocked. For whatever karma we come to live out in this existence is relative to the amount of blockage we receive. It is not to say that if you are unblocked, highly enlightened and self-realized that you won't experience anything undesirable, it only means that you will see everything that happens in a different light.

"Only pure souls of light surround me, none else can be present."

Like the food I eat to nourish my body, the people I AM friends with nourish my soul. I AM mindful of who I chose to be in my life. I'm selective of the energy I surround myself with. We are what we eat and we are who we associate with. Without judgment, I AM mindful of how I interact with people. It doesn't mean if I don't believe the same way or resonate with someone completely that we can't be friends. If every time I AM around someone I feel badly, then I explore the meaning of this person in my life. Sometimes it is necessary to walk away from unhealthy relationships knowing you have loved and done all you can. I pay attention to what it is that I AM learning or providing. In the end, unconditional love is the lesson.

Often people chose to be alone and don't invite others to share in their journey for fear of being judged, ostracized or simply don't want to deal with anyone else's issues or behaviors. I believe that if you are true to yourself and speak your truth, you will attract like souls. Don't ever feel like you are alone. We are all searching for human connection even though we are all connected spiritually. Even if it seems there is nobody that understands you, there is. I had a friend share with me that he is on this planet against his will and struggles with the laws of this creation daily. He has felt alone his whole life and proclaims recollection of all his past lives for millennia. We have had hours of conversation and I've listened to detailed accounts of many of them. His wisdom is ancient, yet he is in his mid 20s. He was ultimately alone on this planet until he wrote a book and shared his story. The book became a best seller. From sharing his truth, he has attracted like souls from all over the planet. He has connected to ancient beings and started a dialog that is infinite in its origins and nurtures his soul. No matter what your story, there is someone to connect with if you share it. Seek out those who can help you on your spiritual journey. Make yourself ready, put yourself out there and connect to those aware and awakening to the collective unconscious.

"Darkness will never enter here, as light will always be."

You read about people being in the wrong place at the wrong time. How can we be mindful to not put ourselves in a dangerous situation? I was out to dinner with my partner when I witnessed two young men with backpacks walk up to the restaurant where we were dining. We were sitting at an outside table and one of the men sat down at the table next to us while the other entered the restaurant and sat down at an empty table where a patron had left food on their plate. He took the plate and then went to several empty tables taking the leftovers to create a full plate of food. He brought it outside where his companion was waiting. The two of them sat and devoured the food while having a disjointed and delusional conversation. I immediately sensed danger and desperation from them. They were discussing life as if it held no value. There was real danger and I sensed their energy was violent. Without tuning closely into what was going on, I could have easily followed my initial thoughts to tell the manager. Who then would have confronted them, causing anger and embarrassment and a series of events that could have created a terrible outcome. They kept looking at me as if to say, "You want to start something?" I quickly shut down my thoughts, began to block their energy and surrounded my partner and I with light. I acknowledged them with a nod and a smile then carried on the conversation with my partner as if they were not there. What my intuition told me was that these two men in their early thirties, nicely dressed and delusional were high on crystal methamphetamine. Their addiction brought them to a dark place, blocking their God receptors and ability to filter the light. I sensed that in those backpacks were drugs, stolen property and a gun. Life meant nothing to them and, in their desperation, would have taken one without regard. By trusting my intuition, I made the right decisions that led to them both leaving without incident. I constantly tune into energy around me. We must be aware of our surroundings at all times. Tune in and you will see that you are given awareness. Always trust your intuition. Let the tape play out in your mind as the information is received.

I was driving home from work one day and stopped at a stoplight. At the crosswalk were a young woman and her friend. She had just finished a bottle of water, looked around, then threw it in the air and it landed in the planter in front of a gas station. Looking uncomfortable, her friend said something to her and she smiled then looked around to see if anyone else noticed. When her eyes met mine, she looked down and walked away. Although she didn't turn around and pick up the bottle, she will remember this interaction the next time she thinks about littering. Although she may not have even cared when she tossed it, the thoughts of all the people who witnessed it hit her hard and created a sense of guilt without a word ever spoken.

Intuition is the transmission and receiving of thoughts and those thoughts can only exist if someone thinks them. I can listen to them or not, but I always trust my intuition.

"Manifestation is one of the greatest gifts we are given, use it wisely."

I believe that one of the most powerful gifts we are given is the ability to manifest things. This same gift can act as our worst nightmare if misused. It is imperative to understand how our thoughts work. With them, we are able to create health, wealth and happiness as well as the opposite if not conscious of what we are thinking and saying. This ancient law has been passed down through generations. While many are aware of the principles of manifestation, they are rarely practiced or quickly forgotten when immediate results are not seen. We may see the law working every day, but not make the connection. If we view life through the filter of this law, we will see examples start to manifest everywhere. We begin to see how we create our existence with every move we make.

I know a man who is by nature angry, but notably with a group of people he feels stole his business unethically. It has consumed his life for years. Every opportunity he has to tell someone about it, he works himself into a frenzy. The more he speaks about it, the angrier he gets. Many have told him he needs to let it go and he can't see that harboring resentment is only hurting him. Every new person he meets hears the story, and each time he tells it, the bad feelings come back and anger permeates his being. Eventually, over time, he developed growths on his vocal chords and was unable to speak loudly enough to be heard. He needed to have surgery and that was not entirely successful. His wife began to suffer from high blood pressure and anxiety.

I know another man who is bitter and lonely and often takes his anger out on those around him. He can be rude, brash and egotistical saying things like, "Don't you know who I AM?" "You don't know what you're doing!"

If somebody does something he doesn't agree with, he snaps and yells at them. Eventually, he developed trigeminal neuralgia, which is very debilitating and rendered him unable to open his mouth to eat or speak. Due to the excruciating pain, he began to avoid daily activities and stopped socializing. He began to lose weight and isolate himself.

Remember the power of every thought you have and action you take.

"I AM love therefore I AM everywhere."

I believe Source is the light which carries unconditional love. Unconditional love is a living, breathing thing. It is everywhere inside, around and infinitely throughout all existence and eternity. When we meditate and bathe in Source, we take unconditional love into our souls. It is healing, soothing, wondrous and pure. It nourishes and speeds our spiritual growth like nothing else. The Source of all existence is simply unconditional love. It is the fundamental energy that gives us life. It is God in all of us. We are everywhere at once and we are love, the perfection of existence. Nothing but love is perfect, yet all else is exactly as it should be. The good the bad, the ups and downs, the struggles and the joy are karma. Every day while deep in meditation I AM overwhelmed by unconditional love and enveloped by golden light that permeates every particle of my being. It is the state of the I AM presence. I stay there as long as I can, basking in the light and listening for whispers. They come like a warm subtle breeze.

"Silence is the realm where most things are learned and understood."

In our busy lives, it is important that we take the time to meditate, still our minds and slow our breathing so we can experience the silence needed to connect to Source and understand our existence. Every one of the Whispers written in this book came at the end of a meditation. As I revisit each one, writing about them is easy and flows naturally from Source with its inherent message. Every day we process thousands of messages. Our thoughts vibrate at light speed as we navigate by our senses through the chaotic energy. Until we slow our breathing and peacefully remove ourselves from the senses, we cannot understand or connect to the spiritual realm. We can learn how to program a television by reading directions, but we can't understand the magnitude of our creation and unconditional love by reading, it must be experienced in silence. There in silence lies the truth of all things. It's programmed in our DNA. Truth-seeking souls unlock the code by deep, frequent and purposeful meditation. Meditation is not complicated. In fact, it's one of the easiest things to learn. However, it does take determination, dedication and practice to still the mind and tune out the senses and thoughts that invade. At the end of this book, I will share the meditation I use every day.

"When you see me looking at you, know that I love you."

If there were one message you could send to every human on the planet, what would it be? When you are observing the world around you, are you judging? Taking in the beauty? Looking for the good or bad in everything? I have found myself doing all the above for most of my life, but mostly judging people's behaviors based on my beliefs. Until I stopped that judgment, I couldn't see the reasons behind them. No two humans think or feel exactly the same. Every soul comes here for different reasons. There may be shared beliefs or learned attributes, but in the soul of the individual lies the program for this life and only he or she has the ability to experience it.

A friend and I were discussing the concept of karma when she became upset about a woman who was raped, "Are you are telling me that she did something to deserve it?" I believe karma comes from past and current life experiences and actions. Sometimes an experience is not only for the one experiencing it, but also for others around them. We never know what someone's past lives entailed nor do we know the absolute truth of their current lives. Karma is simply the sum of a person's actions in this and previous states of existence. It's not a matter of deserve or not deserve it simply is and karma is only one piece of the puzzle.

I try not to judge, practice kindness and compassion, but mostly send thoughts of unconditional love to all. People will feel the energy you put out. What do you want that to be?

"There are dreams which those who never wake, forget."

Everybody has dreams. We may dream for happiness, health and financial freedom to pursue the things that bring us joy. In the moments we are dreaming, we are creator. Creating is the most powerful thing we do as God. We may be lying in bed and thinking about that car we want. We imagine ourselves driving it, the color it will be, the options we want and what it will feel like. We visualize ourselves driving it down the road and can feel the excitement. There is a yearning to have it. We may do the same with remodeling our home or buying new furniture for our apartment. We look through magazines or online and find something we love. We lie in bed at night and imagine what it will be like to live in this new space or sit on our new furniture. We may sit in our living room and look around and imagine where we will place everything, the color of the walls and the fabrics we will use. This is what it means to be a creator. Our thoughts are the most powerful creations on earth. We can virtually create anything we put our minds to. Bringing it into reality is where we falter. This is because, as we imagine the things we want, a little voice in our head tells us we will never be able to get them. So while creating, we are destroying at the same time. We can't do both and succeed. The key is to creating by visualization is to never allow negative thoughts to play out. If ever they appear, immediately replace them with your vision succeeding. Don't allow negative thoughts, they must be destroyed. We need to put our minds in a place where it doesn't acknowledge barriers to our creation. This is a skill we have to learn and it takes relentless practice every day.

Those who do not understand this may dream, yet sabotage those dreams.

"When you accept everything as being perfect, you don't have to be angry anymore."

There are a lot of angry people. They are angry at the world, people, balance of power, not getting their food fast enough in a restaurant, job they have, unappreciated privilege some have, themselves and the list goes on. I hear the word "hate" used all the time. Hate is the most destructive word and thought in our existence. It is the opposite of unconditional love. Why are people so angry? The answer for me seems clear; anger is the absence of understanding everything is as it should be. Everything we experience is solely for our enlightenment. Reflect on what the experience is telling you. There is something important to learn. Our greatest gift is the creator mind. We have the ability to play out the tapes to find meaning in every experience. There is meaning in all karma if we are open to exploring it. Meditating on a given experience does two things, one it opens the door to your heart and enlightenment and two, it burns karma erasing past imprints that bind us. If we take the worst-case scenario of a situation and learn to see the good in it, then it isn't a worst-case scenario any longer. We can find something positive in everything. Every negative can be turned into a positive. We are able to sculpt our existence with our thoughts. Wayne Dyer said time and again, if you change the way you look at things, the things you look at change. The key is to find the true meaning. Look on the bright side. Losing a job means a new opportunity is waiting. Being jobless or homeless might bring spiritual riches that a rich man will never know. Being sick means it's time to relax and take care of yourself. I find that if I think long enough about the things that upset me, I can find the positive meaning in it. But, I have to stop and think, pause and play out the tape, seek first to understand and if something makes absolutely no sense, think again and eventually the truth will reveal itself.

"You are the Creator of the Galaxy called your body. Rule it with unconditional love and light."

Before our souls return to earth we chose our parents. Their DNA allows us to grow into our bodies and gives us the physical blueprint we carry through this life. Everything we experience physically was genetically preprogrammed including how we respond to pathogens, develop and fight diseases and our physical attributes. We chose these bodies to experience exactly what we need to. We also choose how we treat them. Our bodies are an entire universe unto themselves not unlike the one of our stars and planets in their infinite existence. It is planets that are our organs, molecules within the borders of our body where skin meets air, our stars, and other elements in between. If you were an atom, the body would be as big and incomprehensible as our universe. There are countless things going on in our bodies from the existence of peace and harmony, to wars and invasions by entities from inside and outside its borders. From the perspective of an atom, our body is not unlike the stars, planets and space in our own universe. As the atom leaves our body at the point where skin hits the air, it enters another galaxy. This leads to other bodies that have a similar make up as the one they left. This goes on to connect to billions and billions of other bodies and planets each with their own internal universe and all the space in between. Sound familiar? It is a pattern for which all creation exists inside and outside our bodies. Patterns are key in helping us to understand the matrix of our existence. As creator of your own universe, ruler of your body, you chose how to run things. Will you abuse it or nurture it? If the energy you create in your universe is channeled with unconditional love, then the process of manifestation, attraction and karma flow positively.

"Fall into the light, I will catch you. I AM God. I AM the most powerful creator in the universe."

At times while in meditation, the light is so intense that it feels as though I AM free falling at light speed into the infinite arms of the Source at dizzying speeds. At first my reaction is to open my eyes and stop the fall, but as I go with the momentum, I realize that as the most powerful creator in the universe, I trust and therefore I AM safe. I travel infinitely into the living arms of the Source and unconditional love. Here all is known. I dismiss the ego which keeps me bound to body and my existence becomes one with Source.

"Take care of you first for the seeds of love must grow in fertile soil."

Many of us learned at a young age to take care of others before ourselves. Our lives revolve around the need to be acknowledged for our sacrifices. But putting everyone's needs before our own makes us resentful. We cannot find peace until we learn to put ourselves first, love ourselves first and forgive ourselves first. If we surround ourselves with people who don't understand this concept, then we are doomed to have failed relationships, unhappiness and ultimately prolonged karma with life experiences around co-dependency, stress and helplessness. It is a foreign concept for many of us to find comfort from within. Until we take care of ourselves, we will rarely be effective in taking care of others. Until we love ourselves, we are rarely able to unconditionally love others. During meditation one day, a whisper came through that said, "You are here to create a space where others can feel good." I would not be able to do this if I didn't love myself. It's not hard to create this space. Be mindful each time you are interacting with people to create a space where feeling good is easy. Start by asking questions then don't speak, just listen. Try acknowledging, valuing, encouraging them while sending thoughts of unconditional love. This is the space where all can feel good. It is a place where healing can occur.

As my mother-in-law lay in the hospital dying, I had only one thought in my mind and that was to create a loving space where she could feel good about letting go of this body and moving on. One evening as I sat at the foot of her bed, I hummed a beautiful meditation song. As it harmonized with her breathing machine, a harmonic tone filled the room with such richness it vibrated my body. My thoughts were, let go for there is only love to greet you. I filled the hum and my thoughts with unconditional love and sent them into the harmonic vibration that filled the room. This went on for about 15 minutes. I kept repeating in my mind, only love, there is only love. She had not said a word the entire time, but lay with her eyes closed. When I stopped humming, she opened her eyes and said, "This must be the love you are talking about." I was not talking about love, but I sure was sending it. The message got through. I sent this loving vibration to her until her last breath. Then I knew she was free.

"I AM the universe; there will be no wars, only peace in my domain."

In our bodies, our own personal universe, we must stop the battles and wars by creating a place of peace. This is done through loving ourselves and connecting every day to this vast universe in meditation. You are the creator of this existence; rule it with unconditional love and peace. Take care of yourself and nurture the Source that flows through you. In meditation, be mindful of Source flowing through your veins, into your heart, soothing your pain, erasing your bad karma and always loving you, unconditionally. Tears are an elixir, love in pure liquid form. Let them fall down your face, heal your heart and cleanse your soul. I found that the more I meditated, the easier the tears began to flow. All of my years of wall-building slowly began to deconstruct. Slowly over time I became more in tune with my feelings, the universe, Source and to everyone and thing around me. I made a conscious choice to end the wars taking place in my body, mind and spirit. It started with healthy living, exercise, eating right, eliminating negative news and people from my life, daily meditation and practicing putting out into the universe what I wanted to receive back. If you do these things, your life will change.

"Go to the wise ones who have not been clouded by the dark."

This has been one of the most important whispers I have received to date. At what point in our life do we make the conscious decision to change? How do we learn to expand our thinking or decide we are going to elevate our consciousness and begin a spiritual journey? Is it a decision or is it simply fate? If we think back on our lives, how many times did someone say that we had to read a certain book, or watch a show or hear a speaker and we didn't have the time or desire to? These were the moments that the teacher came and the student wasn't ready. When the student is ready, the teacher will come. I have followed Paramahansa Yogananda for years and most recently, Wayne Dyer, Sufian Chaudhary and Godfrey Ray King of the *I AM Discourses*. These men have devoted their lives completely to spiritual understanding and whether you want to call it being gifted, channeling or manifesting, they have brought forth wisdom and astounding revelations to the spiritual meaning of our existence. I have searched my whole life to understand why I was tuned in at a different frequency and these four Masters have revealed to me many of the answers. Teachers come at some point in everybody's life, its up to us to be ready. I believe that it starts with being excited at the possibilities. I AM excited to hear the words of people openly waiting for those pearls of wisdom that will move me forward in my journey. I think that to be consciously aware that teachers are everywhere is key to not missing the signs and opportunities. Listen intently, pay attention to the signs and explore whenever something makes you pause and think. There may be a door that leads to amazing wonders.

I believe it's hard to find original thoughts because we share a collective unconscious. History tells us that every great master had a great teacher. We all inherently know the same truths, but they are covered under layers of karma and clouded by the senses. The masters have been sent to unravel the mystery for us and share the path that eventually we will all be on. With changing times, a new master comes that can speak to the masses. There is nothing new or groundbreaking that they bring other than framing it in a way that most can understand. It has always been the same laws and principles. This book flowed through me from the collective unconscious without a thought given to anything other than the laws being filtered through my own life experiences. My heart and head connected and the revelations flowed onto these pages. I believe the message in this book, and in the books and teachings of others, are all programmed into our genetic code. It lives within our DNA. Once we become activated, it reveals itself and we become compelled to share our story in the hopes it will help someone along their journey. We must choose our teachers wisely. We will know when we find them for our head and heart will connect and agree without a shred of doubt. My litmus test for truth is when my head and heart align perfectly. There are many masters. Each brings a message that, if practiced, can enlighten us and expedite our spiritual journey. The path to enlightenment begins with reading, attending lectures, meditating and expanding our current way of thinking. Since you are reading this book, you are searching. The answers will come if you seek.

I believe that many of today's religions have been corrupted in their interpretation and quest for control. Always keep in the back of your head that religion is another person's interpretation of God, spirituality is your own. Stay true to yourself. You are God. God lives in you. You are the most powerful creator in the universe.

"I move in the space of love, it's everywhere and everything I do."

Being present in our life is a challenge. Conscious awareness of our surroundings, motives and interactions takes discipline. We are heavily inundated by our senses and easily distracted from the moment and synchronistic events continually unfolding. How often are we mindful to really tune into others around us and acknowledge them? It can be a smile, an acknowledgment with a nod of the head, a wave or a friendly hello. We should never be too busy to connect. If we chose not to reach out in some way, then we are isolating ourselves and on many levels disrespecting others. If they chose to not connect, it has nothing to do with you. The air we breathe and the space we move through is made of Source energy. Be present and move consciously through this living unconditional love. Be yourself, be open and be tuned into the love that is everywhere and it will be in everything you do. Slow down enough to feel it. Love is the most powerful energy on this planet. A scowl or dirty look can always be trumped by a smile, wave or loving thoughts. While inside each of us is an unlimited supply of Source energy and unconditional love, for many it is hidden under layers of distraction. If we slow down enough, we will see and feel it in every living thing.

"I connect with every particle of light in the universe. I AM light."

Connecting to light is the fastest way to the Source. When we realize that we are light and can travel at light speed, we no longer have boundaries to limit us. We can travel to the depths of our hearts and minds and everywhere in the infinite universe. It is as simple as a thought. This realization allows me to clearly understand the gifts I have been given in this life. I AM Light and I AM able to be everywhere, in every thought and understand everything. I know the salve that brings the healing and how to shine Source energy into every dark place. When we shine the light of divine love into our thoughts and wishes, we begin to manifest our true purpose and destiny. When we acknowledge we are the light, our energy becomes fuel for those around us. Be a fountain of love for those who are thirsty, let them drink. Help them heal the wounds so that they can love themselves and others unconditionally.

If a person is closed down and blocking the light, then send them love and leave them be. We must remove ourselves from places we are not welcome. We must accept that all are where they should be.

There is a balance between anger and hate, happiness and love. It is this balance that operates the laws of our existence. I refuse to be part of anger and hate and I chose to be happy and loving. I seek to find the silver lining that exists in everything. If we find our way out of anger and hate, we no longer have to be part of the machine that creates and drives it. Remove the things from your life that create anger and hate. Refuse to allow anyone or anything to budge your resolve.

"I AM in awe of the divine presence that surrounds me every day."

When the synchronicities begin to add up and the flame of reality is lit, it is then the divine presence can be seen in full light. It is everywhere and surrounds us at all times. It is this energy that feeds our souls and spiritual journey. When you slow down your breathing and pay attention, you will see the divine presence in everyone and everything. It can bring you to tears. Every synchronicity is a message saying, "Hey, you see, there is something much bigger going on here. We are all connected. Nothing is coincidence." We must only count up the miracles in our lives to see that this is an astounding truth. It doesn't matter where I AM, I see signs everywhere. It can be an overwhelming feeling of gratitude for everything I have causing tears to fall from my eyes from the sheer intensity of it. It can be a thought about my deceased father and a red-tailed hawk lands in a tree right in front of me.

When my mother-in-law was in the hospital dying, there was a Mexican "alebrijes" hummingbird hanging from the ceiling above her. An "alebrijes" is an intricately painted fanciful creation carved from copal wood. She was no longer able to communicate and would stare at it for hours. It seemed that she was putting all of her energy into it and it would turn in circles. She loved hummingbirds and collected photos of them and had them painted on her clothing. One day I was writing and thinking about her when I looked up and directly in front of me was a hummingbird hovering and staring at me. I said, "Hello mama." This happens all the time. There are magical things happening all around us every day.

"Home is where you long to be in the deepest crevices of your soul. You know exactly where that is."

We all define home differently; it could be where we grew up, our mother and father's house or our current residence. Home for me is anywhere I AM sitting in meditation and connecting to the Source. It doesn't matter where. I can close my eyes and instantly become one with the light and travel anywhere in the universe instantly. That can be back to my childhood, Mars, Andromeda, mom and dad's house, absolutely anywhere in the multiverse and infinite realm of existence and my understanding. Home is just a thought made up of particles of light. We can be home anywhere we are. We close our eyes and connect to the Source and there we will find it. I think one of the most profound things I have come to believe is that physical location and the thought of the location are one and the same. If I close my eyes and see myself in my room at home, then even if I AM in another country in a hotel room, I AM in my room at home. The mode of travel is not linear, it is thought. There is no time or space between, it simply is. When I want to travel back to a place I love, all I need to do is think about it and I AM there. I can feel the ground beneath my feat, gentle breezes, sights, sounds and even the scents. I can be anywhere my thoughts take me.

"I AM that in which pure joy flows and light emanates."

I see myself surrounded by pure joy, love and light every day and it makes me smile spontaneously. Many of us are looking for someone or something to bring us joy, yet joy is something that comes from within. Throughout the day I repeat, I AM happy. I think it when I'm walking into a room of people, beginning a meeting, talking on the phone and listening to a conversation. I connect to gratitude or a happy thought and I watch how it grows.

I smile from just thinking about it. If we concentrate on the feeling of being happy, we start to feel joy flowing in our veins. It feels similar to when you are anticipating something wonderful about to happen. It's a feeling of excitement. I work with someone who every time I ask him how he is doing he says, I AM happy and he is. He shines from the inside out and by saying the words he puts out joy to everyone. You can't help but feel good when you are around him. Next time someone asks you how you are doing say, "I AM happy!" Observe how people respond. At first they look stumped, then a smile appears. It's contagious. Be that person in which pure joy flows and light emanates and others will want to drink from the fountain.

"There is no such thing as coincidence, there is divine direction in everything."

We may call it serendipity, synchronicity, uncanny coincidence or a miracle, but it's all the same and it is happening around us every day. It can be as simple as missing the on-ramp to the freeway and having to drive out of your way. You hit every single red light and become annoyed at yourself for missing the on-ramp. But then you learn as you are driving that there was a terrible accident and you not only avoided the traffic it caused, but the potential that it could have been you. But, you are running late and you are supposed to start a meeting promptly at 8 a.m. You hit every red light and every possible thing that can slow you down does. The speed limit is 45 miles per hour on a fast paced two-way road when a semi truck pulls out right in front of you and goes 20 miles per hour with absolutely no way to pass for three miles. There is something trying to slow you down. You left home early so you wouldn't be late and you're getting agitated. The more you get upset the more delays are thrown in your path. At some point it becomes clear that the angrier you are about the delays, the more you are going to draw them to you. It's the law of attraction. You finally get to work ten minutes late and nobody is in the conference room. Why? They were all stuck on the freeway delayed by the accident. So, remember, everything happens for a reason, don't stress the small stuff and go with the flow. It is not the end of the world if you are late for a meeting.

My friend had applied for a job with a company he was very excited about. He put dynamic volition in motion and began his quest to get an interview. He reached out to his contacts on LinkedIn and found a contact that knew the vice president of this company and was willing to give him a good reference and introduction. It all paid off and he was called up and a phone interview was scheduled. He worried about everything going right with the interview and made sure that he had his computer set up and everything was ready with his Bluetooth and earpiece. When the day and time came, he waited as arranged for the VP to call him. He waited, five, ten, fifteen minutes and no call. He couldn't understand why, so he went back and re-read all the emails and discovered that he was supposed to call in to a special number that he had completely overlooked. By the time he did, there was no one on the line. He was mortified. He called the VP's assistant and to his surprise, she apologized that the VP had to miss the call and would set up another time. With a sigh of relief, he was off the hook for not being on the call at the right time. Two more attempts were made to call the VP and both times he neglected to answer. There was always a reason. My friend wouldn't give up and attempted to reschedule the interview one last time. The VP apologized for missing the previous calls and set up a new time. He said he would call this time. My friend had his laptop ready with Bluetooth in ear waiting patiently. Five past the hour, then ten, then thirty minutes went by with no call. Once again let down, he looked through his emails to make sure he had the time and date right, then looked at his phone and realized that the VP had called five past the hour and he missed it. How could this be? He looked at his phone and realized he had placed it on Do Not Disturb mode. Feeling mortified again, he quickly reached out via email to apologize for his gaffe. Two days later, they finally connected and he learned that the position available was one that the VP felt he wasn't qualified for. Two forces at work here. Rather than the VP just telling him this upfront, he put no energy into connecting and therefore the multiple blunders in the process. My friend on the other hand, put so much energy angst into it that he kept creating what he feared most, missing the call or opportunity. The key here is to recognize the signs that the universe is sending you. Trying to force something that doesn't seem right is the worst thing we can do. If we do all the work and it doesn't happen, there are reasons why.

What makes us go against the flow of energy? When obstacles that defy reason are thrown in our path, why do we forge on? Should we push ahead knowing full well we shouldn't? Next time your intuition and reality is telling you contrary to your wishes, pull over to the side of the road and think about it. You might find there is another way to get there or a better place to go.

"I AM pure joy in my perfect creation."

As you reflect upon your journey, take time to think about the experiences you have manifested. Pull them apart and examine each one seeking to understand why and where they took you. Remember that each one has perfectly led you to the next and ultimately where you need to be. In time you will see that the pieces all fit together and the path was divinely orchestrated. Tune in to your creator self and choose to see things in a positive light. Pick the path of kindness and watch as you create the life you want. With practice you will see creation happening in real time with every word you say and every move you make. You will also see that many of the things you have visualized for years are already in your life. Take time to celebrate your creation and your growth. Most importantly, take time to realize, you are the creator. Never forget, you are in control.

"My soul wonders not, it is divinely placed in a crystal glass of sheer perfection."

I AM awake. I never have to wonder for long why things happen in my life. I AM aware of creating in real time. I work seamlessly aside karma knowing there is more than one way to proceed. I don't always take the easiest path, but I know they both eventually lead to the same place. All is perfect, no matter what I believe there is always a silver lining. No matter how painful or hard it all may seem, I never stop trying to understand. While meditating in silence the answers come as whispers or messages from angels or those passed. I have found that if I get stuck and I journal my thoughts then read them to myself, new meaning and understanding comes, often in a flood of unconditional love. Healing begins when our suppressed emotions from long ago connect in real time today. Sometimes just acknowledging what happened, how it felt and offering yourself the unconditional love you needed at the time is enough to burn the karma instantly. The tears? The tears are only love rolling down your cheek. When we take the time to forgive, love and nurture ourselves, we become transparent. When there is nothing left to hide we are truly free.

I think it is human nature to lament over the "what ifs". The more that we tune into these thoughts, the more they consume us and extinguish our light. If ever I find myself doing this, I try to remember that what is done is done. Often there is nothing I can do about it anyway so

I try to find the lesson and move on more enlightened. With each outcome is an opportunity for growth. If it's the best-case scenario, then I thank my lucky stars and remember this is a gift. If it is the worst-case scenario then I AM being pushed to learn something that is essential to my life. Sometimes we cannot make tough decisions so life makes them for us. The important thing to remember when imagining outcomes is to be sure to think positively. Often what we fear the most, we draw to us because there is something there for us to learn. If you find yourself lamenting over the same issue, perhaps there is something that needs further exploration.

"Never abandon hope for in that spark your divine soul lives."

One of the most heart breaking things I have ever seen is when someone abandons all hope. It is the darkest place a human can go. It is at this vulnerable place that a soul may decide they cannot continue to live out karma in this body. Because of my career, I have known people who have committed suicide. Each time it revolved around a life-changing circumstance. Sometimes when an older adult is faced with the prospect of losing independence, they either feel it is too overwhelming to face or they make a sound decision that this is not how they want to live. Back in the late 80s I had a friend who was diagnosed with AIDS and based on what was happening to friends and loved ones around him, he decided he would save himself the ravishes of the disease by putting a gun in his mouth. Choices based on the absence of hope. Being tuned into the ones we love means recognizing the signs that hope is waning. Never let people we love isolate themselves. I believe we should never hold back the words and thoughts of love and how much we care and need them in our life. Hope is the spark of life. If there is no tenderness, warmth or love to feed the soul, hope can die. When we abandon hope, the path becomes dark. Sometimes so dark that no light can come in. Hope is the spark of light that drives our divine soul to Source. At the end of every spiritual Journey we join Source energy. Hope is renewed and we come back again to continue this fantastical journey. No amount of money, not even perfect health can create hope. Hope comes from loving yourself and believing that no matter what, love will sustain you. Never give up hope that you will find that connection with others. There is an unlimited supply of love on this planet, take solace in knowing that it starts with you. Once you know that, remember to take your hand, place it over your heart and caress it repeating, I love you, I AM loved, believe it and never forget it. Create a habit of connecting to this self-love every day and as much as you can. You can only nourish yourself by doing so. Never abandon hope for this is where our creator self is born. Hope is the path and love is the light.

"Let go of your past perceptions of reality, the truth lays in your intuitive heart."

As we go through our day, we remember that perceptions we have may in fact be based on past experiences that have no relevance to what is happening now. Is it relevant today? One of the most powerful gifts is intuition. Work on developing it, trusting it and connecting it to your actions in ways that will help guide you through life. In developing our intuition, we learn to trust the inertia behind every action of our creation. Filter out the noise of past relationships to find the current relevance. As we go through life, scars build and cause us to be jaded or cynical. Try to see past people's actions and into the core of them. Sometimes there are opportunities for growth and healing for all. Don't be afraid to find that innocence again. Not everyone is out to hurt us.

"Ego demands love for all the wrong reasons."

Ego is one of the most powerful forces on earth. It divides and conquers. It is the root of all evil. Those with the biggest egos dominate and run our planet. Lust for power, control, money and sex become the focus. This focus is the antithesis of our spiritual nature. The natural foe of ego is love. For not all the power, riches, fame and glory in the world can win the true love of another. When ego demands love and love is not returned, ego becomes unstable. This instability is the root-cause of wars, divorces, destruction of lives and businesses. How do we learn to identify and understand our ego? Ego says, "They will never find someone better than me." Love says, "I cannot control what another person feels, let them go with love for I love myself and will be strong without them." Ego says, "How dare they disrespect my family!" Love says, "This is not about my family, this is about them. I will nurture and love my family and they will create from the seeds they have sown." Ego says, "But why am I not good enough for them?" Love says, "I AM good enough and I love myself. I move on peacefully with love and acceptance that this is not about me." Acceptance is the answer to bridging ego and love. We can only give love. We cannot demand it. If by giving love, love is returned, then it is the greatest gift of all.

"When your souls higher purpose is activated, love blows like a gentle breeze everywhere you step."

As we journey through this life and live out our karma, there comes a time when we ask ourselves, is this all there is? We instinctively know that it is time. Ultimately it comes for everyone. I'm not going to tell you that it will happen in this lifetime. But it will happen. Years of searching takes us on an amazing quest and then just like that, we know there is a higher purpose. Everyone arrives here. No one is exempt. Conscious contact with God for just an instant creates activation. The quest will take on twists and turns until the day we arrive at the end. There before you is a living breathing answer to every question you have ever asked. By now you know the answer, love is the answer. You will begin to feel love, breath love and make love your quest. There isn't a single person we walk by that isn't programmed with unconditional love. They may not be activated, but they will be. We are all walking around each at a different vibration of self-realization. Some are new on the journey and others advanced and moving fluid through their day. When we begin to see the love in everyone, we feel it emanating from even the most negative person we encounter. It is our very nature to love and be loved all else is a façade which cascades across our true purpose.

"I AM the water, the air, the clothes you wear, the car you drive, I AM every particle everywhere, I AM alive."

When I think of the physics of our existence and all the particles of energy that move around us, I think of how miraculous it is that they are able to form together when filtered through some genetic code, to create our human body. It isn't hard to believe that we are all connected by these particles vibrating simultaneously through us. We may be separated from each other by empty space however; this empty space is full of even more particles of energy. These particles make up everything on this planet from rocks to humans and they exist in all the empty spaces between. If you were to break down our bodies into particles and spread them out on a screen, you would only see tiny sparks of light. Then if you pull it all together in the right sequences, you can miraculously form everything that exists on this planet. The smallest measurable particles such as electrons and quarks and still yet to be discovered smaller particles can be broken down infinitely smaller. Conversely the big bang theory proclaims that the known universe of particles keeps expanding outward infinitely. These two opposite ends of the spectrum are exactly the same and create the very definition of infinity. We are omnipotent, everywhere and everything at once. We move fluidly throughout infinity for we are God.

"You are forgiven by the nature of forgiving yourself. Nobody else needs to."

Guilt is a powerful force in our lives. We may spend an entire lifetime beating ourselves up and feeling bad for things we should or should not have done. We may hope others forgive us our transgressions, but it is not always possible. More healing and powerful is forgiving our self. There is a very profound lesson behind guilt, one that will reveal itself when meditated upon. We have been conditioned all our life to feel guilt based on social norms, morals, rules and religion, but in reality guilt most always comes from disrespecting ourselves. Ultimately, only we know the truth behind our guilt. There is no preachy morality here. We only need to tune into the acts that are causing us to feel guilty and if they don't resonate with our higher purpose, then they are probably happening to teach us something. Pay attention to what that is. Beating ourselves up is the most damaging thing we can do. Negative self-talk, name-calling and self-loathing digress our soul. It creates and attracts the very things we feel badly about and brings to fruition our greatest fears. We should embrace ourselves, touch our hearts and speak loving things to our soul. Know that we are God and perfect in our creation. Nobody needs to forgive us for anything. We need only to forgive ourselves.

"If ever you get lost seek first to find me, I AM everywhere inside you."

I was taught at a young age that God was outside of me, a benevolent being who lived in heaven and protected me from harm and evil only if I agreed to live by the rules of the bible. As a child I lay in bed each night and prayed to this God to protect me from monsters and please stop the earthquakes. I believed that God was the only source that could protect me. Since I feared monsters and earthquakes so much, they seemed to appear at regular intervals in Los Angeles during my childhood. Looking back it is profound that I created what I feared and my beliefs couldn't have been further from the truth. As a child I would never have imagined I would come to believe one day that I AM God. I can see clearly now looking back to when I first saw the particles of light bouncing off the minister's head, he wasn't just a man preaching about another's interpretation of God, he was a man unaware that he was God talking to Gods. This was the only truth in the room.

"Respect and emanate the light in everything for it is the very breath you breathe."

The very air we breathe is made up of particles of light and energy and is as important as the food we eat. Breathe it in and feel your soul alive and awakened. We are pure Source incarnated into body. I have often wondered how the light works within the matrix of our existence. I think of my ability to be inside the thoughts of others and see specific events that shaped their life. The very particles that emanated from the minister's head and shoulders carry the thoughts and memories via vibration directly into the synapses of my brain. It is by these very particles of light that we are all connected. Why I AM able to download others memories is a gift. I understand the fluid movement of particles between us. This is the only explanation for telepathy. With each breath we take, we draw in life force, light and Source. When we exhale and release this energy, we send back love.

"Accept everything as Divine perfection."

As we find ourselves upset about things not going the way we want, remember to find the reason. Don't let it build up. Embrace it and move on. There are no mistakes.

Everything is exactly how we create it. Nobody has the ability to create in our lives but us. Our thoughts and choices are responsible for our experience. We might ask why someone is born into the slums of an undesirable place with a terrible quality of life. The answer is simple, because it is exactly the way it is supposed to be. We must never judge our existence against another's. There is something to learn in every existence and experience. It is up to us to figure out what that is. Many live life in an orgy of the senses that blocks out the light and its ability to transcend our existence from slave to God. The higher we develop our spiritual selves by frequent meditation and detachment from the senses, the more we unlock the DNA given by our creator. As we learn to accept everything as divine perfection, we begin to see that whatever we attract in our lives, both good and bad are here to teach us something.

I know a woman who had been working at the same organization for many years. She worked hard, lived the company culture, was honest, ethical and had been very instrumental in turning around a failing business all the while keeping morale up even during the worst of times. She told me that she believed that by working hard, she would get recognized as someone to develop and promote. After many successful years she began to ask her supervisor for more responsibility repeatedly asking what she needed to do to be seen as ready to promote. Her boss would agree to give her more responsibility but there was never any follow-up. It seemed the more she asked, the further her boss pushed her away. She worked harder and tried harder to great success yet to no avail. She tried hard to not take it personally as she watched people around her get the opportunities she desired. Each year she received an excellent review and in the comments section would express her desires to further her career. Still nothing. Her disillusionment was strong until reality hit her upside the head. She realized if she was doing all the right things and knocking on the door over and over but nobody was answering, then it was time to accept where she was at or move on. She finally realized that everything happens for a reason and in order to grow sometimes you have to step outside of your comfort zone. Her disillusionment turned to excitement when she left the company for a big promotion. The lesson here is to read the signs and trust your intuition. For whatever reason, she was not being groomed for a promotion. For a long time she failed to acknowledge this reality. Sometimes moving outside of our comfort zone is the fastest way to success.

"Our mind is an instrument that must be tuned daily."

Our brain is the most amazing biochemical masterpiece ever created. It is the command center for our body and soul and the receptor of all energy within the universe. It is an antenna that transmits and receives everything we need to complete our programmed existence here on earth. At some point along the journey we are given the opportunity to activate, learn and understand the laws of the universe. We are given enlightenment to understand the programming of the matrix and our destiny. We may also be destined to be a slave to our senses. I think if you are reading this book, that is not your destiny. Each of us has the ability to tune out our senses. They do not have to rule us. While we may need them to navigate the waters of existence on this planet, they can be tuned out and fine-tuned to bring us closer to enlightenment. In order to do this, we have to learn how to tune them out so we can connect with Source. Levels of consciousness are tuned like an instrument. To hear a perfect C chord on the guitar, the instrument has to be tuned and you have to know how to place your fingers on the frets to make the note. Same with the mind, it is an instrument that needs to be tuned daily during meditation in order to receive the pathway that allows us to connect to Source. Without tuning our minds, we cannot achieve enlightenment and will never truly break free of the senses that bind us. Love makes the most beautiful music. Tune your instrument and feel it. Let the love spill out of your eyes for this is the beauty of life. Relish it.

My boss had taken me out to lunch at a seaside café one day and we were discussing our management team. For some reason, I knew she was going to tell me one of them was ill. Before she could, I told her that Sue was not well and I sensed it was something about her blood. She looked at me and said, "Did she tell you she has leukemia?" she had not, I just knew it. I was still reeling from the news and the fact that I already knew it and my boss was a little taken aback. I had sensed she wasn't well for some time and I must have picked up on my boss' thoughts. Either way, I felt sharply tuned to energy this day. When we left the restaurant, we got to the car and my boss had locked the keys in the console. You could see them through the window and she explained that her spare set was at home 15 miles away. She decided to call AAA and see if they could open the door and retrieve the keys. About 20 minutes later they arrived and could not get the door open. It was a Volvo with strong anti-theft measures built in. I remember thinking, if I can use my energy to pick up on someone's illness or read someone's thoughts then why couldn't I use this same energy to open the door. I told my boss this very thing and she laughed at me. I placed my hand over the key slot on the door and shot a blast of energy into it while repeating, "Open, open, open." each time shooting more energy into the keyhole. Just as the AAA driver was preparing to tow the vehicle, I shot one last blast of energy, I heard a click and then all the doors unlocked. I quickly reached in, grabbed the keys and walked over to the tow truck where my boss and the driver were standing. I dangled the keys at them and said, "I got them." They both looked at me puzzled and I told my boss I would explain later. We talked about it at length on our way back to work and I'm not sure she ever really believed me. It was just another confirmation and it is not likely I could do it again. But, who knows. Our mind is an instrument and can perform miracles.

"I AM in your heart in an instant permeating your soul with divine light."

Once our instrument is tuned, we can call upon Source at any time to still our minds, calm our hearts, nourish our bodies and help us move fluidly through the day. With practice we become virtuosos in instantly feeling love, peace and harmony. Remember it is unconditional love, light and Source that allow us to breathe, live and exist in peace on this planet. Choose to dull your senses with presence of mind, do not react, observe and choose. We are not these bodies we are divine love. While in these bodies we long for touch, companionship, and sensuality, creation itself. We long for someone or something to love when the answer is to love ourselves.

"I will not be ruled by the emotions in my human heart."

If we allow them, emotions can be powerful. On one hand they can create intense beauty on the other drama, chaos and addictions. We should never let our emotions rule us, but rather tame and reframe them. Intense emotions have been responsible for creating the world's most beautiful art, music and literature. Love, elation, chaos, heartbreak, fear and pain are a muse for many and they will manifest it over and over for their art. I think of two of the most influential artists of my generation, Prince and Michael Jackson. Both incredibly talented men, both addicted to drugs, both died of an overdose.

The list of great artists who have succumbed to addiction is too long. They crossed the line between being master or slave to their emotions. I think of my friend Lorraine who died from addiction issues. She had years of recovery with the help of the 12-step program written by Bill Wilson. In this book the author talks about hitting bottom, the lowest place you can go, where the only place to go is up. He said addicts would not change until their pain got great enough and then sometimes it's too late. He said to have recovery from addiction we have to admit that there is a power greater than ourselves and believe that this power can restore us to sanity. I believe this can also mean discovering that greater power is you or your higher self. He talked about an incredible experience he had which has incidentally helped millions of addicts around the world. According to Bill W. while lying in bed totally depressed and desperate he cried out, "I'll do anything! Anything at all! If there be a God, let Him show Himself!" He said he experienced a bright light that suddenly created a feeling of ecstasy and then serenity. This was his activation. He was ready. It is reported that he never drank again for the rest of his life. I believe that while addiction is complex, it is mostly emotions out of control, unbearable pain. It could be addiction to anything, gambling, sex, drugs, alcohol, eating and smoking. If we numb out by using whatever means, then we don't have to feel the emotion, the substitute takes its place. If we share our emotions with someone safe and nonjudgmental and learn to understand and feel them, they will become more bearable. If we understand and accept our emotions we can bring addictions under control and create recovery. This is all part of fine-tuning our instrument. Chose love over anger, fear and pain. Chose to accept and forgive daily. Everything will be fine. No matter what comes our way, we are the higher power and we create our lives every day.

"Perfect stillness and Light, I AM one with you. Source of unconditional love, I AM your echo."

It was not long after I read Sufian Chaudhary's book *World of Archangels* that my spiritual journey accelerated. It seemed as though I was traveling at light speed activated by the Source of his message. I wanted to meet this man. I wanted to share with him the dream I had in Hawaii after reading his book. I wanted to tell him how his book spoke to my heart and what a gift it was. Mostly I wanted to share the miraculous confirmation I received and tell him I believed in him and his light. I began to add Sufian into my meditations each day. When I came to the part where I visualize the people I want in my life, he was at the table along side Wayne, Oprah and Deepak. For two months I visualized this until one day I looked up Sufian's book online. It led me to his Facebook page and I sent him a friend request. To my astonishment, he immediately accepted. It was very late, but I sent him this message, "Thank you for accepting my request. I'm just retiring to bed, but want to share an amazing event that happened after I read your book. I'll write soon.

You are a very old soul, my friend, nice to connect with you in this life." He responded, "Hi, no problem at all. I look forward to chatting!" This was the beginning of our friendship. We connected as ancient souls reunited. Hours of conversation ensued. I feel certain that by visualizing him daily, I manifested him in my life. Sufian put out his story and attracted like souls to his circle. Something he knew he needed to do. He is an ancient soul, an ascended master from multiple dimensions and has been placed here on earth to create a light bridge to guide souls towards Source and unconditional love.

I told Sufian many times that he needed to meet Wayne Dyer because I somehow felt that they would do something great together. I knew that Wayne would take Sufian under his wing if they ever met or Wayne read his book. It was a few months after Sufian and I became friends that I went to Hawaii on vacation. I discovered through a Facebook posting that Wayne was giving a talk at a hotel right next to mine. The title of the weekend was "I AM Light". I couldn't believe the synchronicity of him speaking at the same time I was there and I quickly signed up. It could not be coincidence and I knew that I needed to meet him and tell him about Sufian. I knew Wayne would love Sufian and want to share his incredible message as he does with so many amazing people. On the first day of the talk, I was sitting in the front of the room directly behind Wayne's personal assistant, his wife and two of his children. I was amazed that the universe put me there as I had been meditating that I would meet him every day for months. At one point, his wife went up on stage and he came and sat less than a foot directly in front of me. Yet even in this close proximity, it wasn't the time to meet him. Whenever there was an opportunity, a long line of people appeared. I just didn't feel the time was right. Yet, his personal assistant was sitting right in front of me so during a break I took the opportunity to introduce myself and tell her about Sufian and his book. I told her that Wayne would love it and I hoped she would give him the note I made on the back of a napkin with Sufian's name and book title. I wished I had a copy to hand deliver. She said she would give it to him. I believe to this day that she did. How could all of this happen if not to introduce Sufian's book to him? I felt that I would meet him through Sufian so never made the effort to stand in line for a meet and greet.

At one point during Wayne's presentation, he called his wife Marcelene up on stage to lead a meditation. I sat in the audience looking up at her on stage and poured every ounce of energy I had into sending her love. When the meditation concluded, she returned to her seat, which was directly in front of me. She turned around and said, "I want to let you know that I felt your love." I smiled and said, "You're beautiful and I could feel your love." It was yet another confirmation that this incredible alignment was happening. I was happy that she felt the love and even more that she said something. I know that I manifested this miraculous string of events. To this day, Wayne has not reached out to Sufian. This was five months ago. I know that all of this synchronicity has set a ball in motion for all of us to meet one day. There can be no other reason that all of this happened. I AM Light was the name of Wayne's talk, this whisper made me think of being Light and creating the amazing path that took me to Wayne that weekend as well as introduce me to my dear friend Sufian. As I edit this book, I find myself here at this whisper now knowing that Wayne has passed on. It is interesting to know that this may be the reason he never reached out to Sufian and also that while I was not able to manifest this meeting in person, it doesn't mean that they will not meet. I still have Wayne in my meditations. He now sits at the alter with the many Masters I call upon for guidance. I love you Wayne and you speak to me every day.

"Take the steps one at a time and focus on the stillness that is unconditional love."

It can be difficult in our busy lives to find the time to develop our spirituality. Yet if we don't take the time, we will remain trapped and ruled by the world of our senses. By design our senses are intoxicating. They constantly distract us and can make it difficult to learn meditation, which is essential to spiritual growth. But all we have to do is decide to make a change. It starts there. Creating a habit takes 21 days. Make a commitment to get up 30 minutes early every day to meditate. The process of mediation activates our DNA and enlightenment unfolds. It is the single most important thing we can do.

I promise that if you do this one thing every day, your life will change. When we take time each day to still our minds and connect with our God-self, we begin elevating our consciousness. Get online and search for meditation music. Pick something that resonates with you. The music from Wayne Dyer's I AM Wishes Fulfilled Mediation is stunning. Sit down in a quiet place in your home, get comfortable, close your eyes and connect with the Source; in time, you will be one with the living golden light of unconditional love. Be patient, it will come and when it does your life will never be the same.

"I AM insight upon my path of creation."

As our consciousness expands and we become more aware of our true God-self, the connection to Source can be instant. As simple as a shift in our thoughts to a place we arrive at in mediation where we feel bliss, oneness and Source within us. This connection will guide us through day-to-day obstacles and give us understanding into the meaning of energies around us if we are tuned in, listen and trust our intuition. Ultimately the true meaning in everything that happens and what it means becomes clear. As we begin to focus on our day and every encounter, let it unfold in slow motion, look for insights and understanding and be mindful to create your reaction carefully and watch the outcomes. You will begin to see how powerful you are. How we react to everything is within our control. As time goes on and with practice, we become masters of our own existence.

By the time we are finished here on earth, we return to spirit and ready ourselves for the next beautiful chapter of our lives.

"Breath is what takes stillness of matter and gives it life. I AM the breath the resurrection and the life."

As we become more advanced in our meditation and learn to control our breath, we can see the deeper purpose it has in our very existence. On this planet, we cannot exist without the air we breathe. It is the essential life-giving source and the glue that holds the particles of our body together. When we no longer breathe, our body dies and immediately begins to decay. As we focus on the breath going in and out, we begin to see that it is not only essential to life, it is also the way we take in everything that is around us. Every particle we breathe into our lungs is a part of the infinite multiverse that we live in. It nourishes our bodies and is solely responsible for keeping us alive. It is the pure essence of life, as we know it. It is unseen yet fluid in its form and purposeful in its creation. We work symbiotically with its function. It cannot exist without us, as we cannot live without it. If there were nothing on this planet that needed oxygen, would it exist? At one time we were rocks, it wasn't until we breathed in oxygen that we became alive in the third dimension. I AM the breath of the universe.

Jesus said, "I AM the resurrection and the life. Anyone who believes in me will live, even after dying." When I was 16-years-old, I met a stigmata. A stigmata is a person who bears the wounds of Jesus Christ. My uncle was friends with Victor Emmanuel Wenzel von Metternich and his wife Elena. They frequented my uncle's deli in Montrose and they became close friends. Victor and Elena were instrumental in getting the story of Padre Pio made into a movie. They gave my uncle the gift of a piece of Padre Pio's scarf with a bloodstain on it. He kept it on the bedside table in his bedroom and would often show it to me with great reverence. The first time he showed it to me he said, "You see how it is a completely white cloth? Tomorrow you will see a blood stain appear." and it did. There were days the cloth was completely white and others where you could see the stain. My uncle and Padre Pio shared the same birthday of May 25th and my uncle felt a strong connection to him. During the 70s a young woman by the name of Ivana was living with Victor and Elena. The Catholic Church was investigating her for her claim of bearing the Stigmata. The church was reticent to accept her claim for she had a child, but they had been investigating and following her for many years. My uncle wanted badly for my father and I to meet her and receive a blessing. My father agreed and we were invited to Villa Elena to meet her. Arriving at the estate, the gate was closed so we parked on the street outside. Upon exiting the car, the smell of roses permeated the air. My uncle met us at the gate and led us into the house and to the kitchen where Ivana was sitting in a chair, head, hands and feet wrapped in bandages each with blood stains on them. The smell of roses continued to permeate the room. My uncle said it was her blood. In Italian, he asked if she would bless us. One at a time we kneeled before her, she took our hands in hers and prayed. I didn't really feel anything at the time, but the smell of roses was so strong it was overpowering. My uncle insisted that we stay for dinner but my father wanted to take me out so we left. When we returned to the car, the tire was flat. It took me about thirty minutes to change it and my hands were filthy. I could still smell roses on my hands through the grime and oil smells. When we got to the restaurant, I went to the bathroom and scrubbed my hands intensely with soap and water to remove the dirt and grime. While I was able to get them clean, the smell of roses was still strong. In bed that night, I could not stop smelling the roses. In fact, the smell remained on my hands for over a week and on my pillow for over two weeks. I don't know why other than my uncle telling me it was her blood. The day after we met her, my father took the tire in to be repaired. The mechanic said, "There was nothing wrong with it, I just filled it with air." My uncle and aunt shared stories of Ivana being tormented by demons and witnessed her wounds open and close before their very eyes. He was convinced that is why we had a flat tire.

"Through my manifestations I AM the dreams fulfilled."

As we create and sculpt our reality, wishes and dreams with our thoughts, we are also contributing to the reality of others. Whether or not we consciously know it, everything we manifest in our lives has a direct effect on those around us. Take for instance the parents that invest and save every penny they ever made and hide their riches and their daughter who dreams of financial freedom, inherits it. In the process of manifesting your destiny you are actually impacting the destiny of others. It is an incredible cycle that plays out within the laws of our creation. We exist in a symbiotic relationship with everyone ebbing and flowing fluidly in perfect harmony, co-creators in a sea of unlimited potential. Nothing is quite as it seems as the laws and energy spin our thoughts into reality.

I saw a video on Facebook filmed with a body cam strapped to a police officer capturing him shoot an unarmed man. When I first saw it, I was horrified. The article said that the man didn't hear or heed the officer's warnings because he had headphones on. It was a violent, extremely sad, shocking death and a terrible tragedy for all involved. The district attorney in the case ruled that the killing was justified in that the officer reasonably perceived his life was being threatened. The officer expressed fear. He truly believed that the man was going to shoot him and he was going to die. It was revealed during the trial that the 20-year-old man had written the following words in the days leading up to his death, "I feel my time is coming soon, my nightmares are telling me. I'm gonna have warrants out for my arrest soon ... I'll die before I go do a lot of time in a cell." "I finally realize I hit rock bottom. I'm homeless I haven't slept in two days ... as I walk through this valley of the shadow of death I AM fearing evil. It's about my time soon." It is a tragic series of events that changed the life of the officer, the young man, his family and friends and anyone who reads his story. In the realm of energy, our thoughts are the most powerful thing we have as Creators. Negative thoughts, fear and perseveration on them are the movie you will project onto the screen of life. Remember this profound revelation.

"I need nothing more than to be one with the Source."

While I consciously decide daily to surround myself with positive thoughts and energy, I AM still living in the matrix with its many cosmic and karmic variations. Sometimes during my meditations as I AM connecting with my purpose, my family and Source, I sometimes find it hard to open my eyes and go on with the day. I could sit in meditation for hours. The longer I meditate, the more blissful I become. The silver lining is that when I do finally open my eyes and go on with the day, grace comes from the residual effects. It allows me to be aware in the moment and an observer moving fluidly around the drama. I AM reminded daily that I AM here for one reason, to love.

I prefer to be in conscious contact with Source and I need nothing else but that unconditional love emanating its golden light through every particle of energy in existence.

"It is gravity that pulls you to the Source, any effort otherwise will result in pain and suffering. Surrender to the pull."

Gravity is not only here to keep us on the ground, it is a powerful force which pulls us toward Source. It is our natural gravitation. While we are being called many times a day, week, month or lifetime to elevate our consciousness we may still defy gravity, turn the other way and struggle. It is our destiny to experience what we came to learn. Do not resist the gravity that pulls you toward the Source. Open your mind and heart. Read that book someone recommended, check out that website and search for the truth. Once you make up your mind to do it, you will never look at life the same.

"There is purpose in everything that happens."

I hear a lot of conspiracy theories around vaccines and whether or not to take them. Many parents are refusing to allow their children to receive them much to the anger and ridicule of the medical world that has seen a rebirth of old diseases such as measles, mumps, chicken pox and polio. I can't take vaccines because they cause me to have heart arrhythmias. Doctors have yet to be able to explain why this happens, nonetheless it is well documented in my medical records. While attending a business function in early 2000, the attendees were offered free pneumonia and flu vaccines. Without even thinking about it, I decided I would take them up on it. One shot in each arm and it was over or so I thought. Later that night I began to feel weak and experienced dizziness and light-headedness. I decided to go to bed early. I could feel my body's immune system kicking into overdrive as it began to fight and build antibodies to the multiple dead viruses and bacteria injected into me. That night I woke up with a very unusual heart rhythm. It would race then would suddenly slow down to a normal rhythm then start up again with each deep breath I took. While it worried me, I decided to try and sleep it off. By morning, my heart was not only racing, it began skipping, pausing and at times stopping. At this point I was afraid so I rushed myself to the emergency room. While at the check-in window a nurse overheard me telling my symptoms to the clerk and rushed out to take my pulse. Without even checking me in, they immediately brought a wheelchair, wheeled me into a room and a doctor was at my side in seconds. At this point I was hooked up to a monitor and had an IV in my arm. I told the doctor that I had two vaccines the day before and these strange rhythms started happening shortly after and I could create them by holding my breath or lying in certain positions. He told me that it wasn't possible to control or change my heart's rhythm at will to which I told him, "Oh yeah, watch." With that, I took a deep breath and my heart began to beat irregularly and it was then he jumped to attention and called for help. Quickly I had a team of doctors and nurses at my side watching the monitors as I created this impossible phenomenon. "OK, make it happen again." And I did, over and over. I was injected with different drugs in an attempt to determine where the rhythm was being generated. Still, no success yet I continued to be able to create it with breath and positioning. Several tests later the doctors started to look worried. I was told they were going to do a trans-esophageal echocardiogram. I was in a stupor when one of the doctors got close to my ear and whispered, "I suspect that you might have a growth or a tumor in your heart causing this." He told me it could be that when I laid back and took a deep breath that a growth or something was pressing into my heart and positioning itself in a way that caused a blockage of the electrical pathways or the flow of blood in my heart. He explained they were going to put a device down my throat into my esophagus that would create an image by bouncing sound waves off my heart. They would be able to see if there is anything unusual. If they saw something dangerous, they would want to remove it immediately. He wanted my permission to do surgery if needed. He asked, "Do we have your permission?" If I was scared to start, now I was terrified. My mind raced. I started playing out the scenarios and images in my head. They will knock me out, hook me up to a machine, cut open my chest, open my heart, remove the growth and I will wake up with a big scar down the middle of my chest where they split me open. Worse, I thought, maybe I'll die on the table. As my anxiety level increased, I began to panic and hyperventilate. I felt the same way I did on the fire line that day and thought I was going to die. I just wanted to pass out and have it be over. As tears began flowing out of my eyes, a rush of calming energy came over me. I began to tingle and I felt myself leaving my body. I slowly rose above the bed and flipped around until I felt my back against the ceiling. I opened my eyes and was looking down on myself lying in the hospital bed. In that moment, I heard a voice saying, "Gary don't be afraid. You just step into the light." "You cannot die." In that moment the fear began to subside. My heart and my head connected to this truth. If I were to die, I would just step into the light.

I spent four days in the hospital undergoing every cardiac test known including an electrophysiology study. They could find absolutely nothing wrong with my heart or me. In later years my doctor would tell me that it was caused by the flu shot and that I had a disorder that didn't allow me to properly process the proteins in the vaccine. Whether or not this was true, I will never know. The lesson I learned from this experience was clear, I was no longer afraid to die. As the gravity of the situation pulled me to the Source, I let go. I let love heal me on every level of my existence. The message was clear; I AM the energy that lives in your body. I AM not your body. I only attach to feel, experience and know things of the physical realm. I have always been and will always be. You cannot die.

"I AM not this body I AM the space in this room that always was and always will be."

I have had four out-of-body experiences in this life. The first was on the fire line, the second after my pneumonia and flu vaccine. The third was when I was attending college at Humboldt State University. I had just come home from a long day of classes and was exhausted. I went directly to my bedroom, threw my backpack on the floor, jumped on the bed and fell into a deep sleep so fast that I recall the process of it. I closed my eyes and instantly realized that I was asleep, yet awake. It was as strange place between consciousness and dream state. As I realized I was dreaming yet fully conscious, I tried to get up from the bed, but couldn't so I pushed what I can only call "my soul" out of my body and began to float up to the ceiling much the same way I did when I was in the hospital with arrhythmia. When I reached the ceiling, I flipped around and my back was flat against it. When I looked down, I could see myself on the bed below. I was amazed that I was out of my body and able to float through the air and actually see my sleeping body. It was the most exhilarating feeling. I turned around with my stomach against the ceiling and by sheer will I pushed myself through the ceiling into the condo above me. There wasn't anyone home, but I floated around in energy form through the living room. I went into each bedroom and into the kitchen. I even opened the refrigerator and freezer and could see the contents of beer, left-over food in containers and nothing but ice in the freezer. I decided I would float up through the roof and take a peek outside. I pushed my way through the ceiling and roof and found myself outside in the pouring rain. As the cold water hit me, it jolted me awake. As I slowly opened my eyes with full recollection of what just happened, I realized it was pouring outside. I had been asleep for about 15 minutes.

The fourth time I had an out-of-body experience was when I was living in Santa Rosa with my friend Eduardo. I was very tired and went into my room to take a nap. I fell fast asleep and realized that I was in that place between being conscious and dreaming. Again, I pushed my soul out of my body and floated up to the ceiling, my back against it looking down at myself. The process I describe as pushing my soul out of my body is one that I have experienced several times. I can compare it to holding your breath and bearing down. In my out-of-body experiences I believe that my soul leaves the flesh. This time I floated down from the ceiling and drifted through the air into the living room. I noticed through the sliding glass door a strange glowing light coming from outside. I pushed myself toward the door and then through the glass and outside onto the balcony. Above me I could see blue sky full of puffy little clouds. As I watched them floating peacefully in the sky I started to hear the sound of trumpets blowing. I felt goose bumps all over my body.

As I looked around I began to see people floating up into the sky. They were rising from the streets, cars and out of apartment windows. The clouds began to part and there in golden rays of light was Jesus floating in mid-air with his arms outstretched. In my excitement I yelled, "Eduardo, quick, come here, Jesus has come for us, we're going home." I raised my open arms to the sky and began to float upward. Just before I reached Jesus, I jolted awake. In utter amazement with full recollection of my dream, I jumped out of bed and ran out in the living room to tell Eduardo what just happened. As I entered the living room I saw the golden glowing light beaming through the sliding glass door. I quickly opened it and went outside. There in the sky above me was the very same puffy clouds from my out of body experience. My hair stood on end and I said out loud, "Eduardo, Jesus is coming."

In our world of infinite energy particles we are but a mass illusion of form held together by invisible forces to create a projected reality onto the screen of life. Nothing is real or as it seems. We are made of the same particles of energy that exist in the chair we sit in, the clothes we wear, the air we breathe and dirt in our garden. The space between the wall and us is filled with these same particles and while our senses trap us into a false reality the truth is clear, we are not our bodies; we are one with everything that exists in the infinite multiverse.

"The realities of time and space and are an illusion, we live forever."

I remember clearly when my father was in his early sixties I was spending the night at his house and was jolted awake in the middle of the night to his screams for help. He was having a bad nightmare as he often did from posttraumatic stress disorder. I jumped from my bed and went into the hallway. I found him in the bathroom at the sink. I'll never forget the way he looked at me and almost in a whisper said, "Son, if I ever get dementia, you have to shoot me." He was serious. This was his way, but I only shook my head and said, "Papa, I AM not going to shoot you." and he said matter of fact, "Then get me a gun and I'll do it myself." As the years went by and my father aged into his late seventies, signs began to appear that his cognition was slipping and eventually he was diagnosed with dementia. I had oversight of his care for nearly ten years. As his dementia progressed and he became more dependent, I watched as his greatest fears began to unfold. He chose me as his power of attorney for everything because he trusted me and knew I would always uphold his wishes. Up to the final days of his life, whenever he would see me he would light up and though unable to form words would babble and smile love at me. I knew what he was saying, "Hey, son of mine!" Something he always said whenever he saw or spoke to me. I received a call from his doctor one morning telling me that he had pneumonia and it would likely take his life unless treated. My father demanded that I not prolong his life in any way and made it perfectly clear in his power of attorney for healthcare. He had survived ten years against the odds with near perfect health. It was the hardest decision I have ever had to make, but I knew what my father wanted. I told the doctor no. His dementia was to the point where he was aspirating his food and next steps would be tube feedings, which are the kind of heroics he strictly forbid. I told the doctor that I wanted to keep him comfortable with absolutely no pain. His oxygen levels were in the 80s and even with continuous oxygen he was irritable. It took a short time to get him comfortable on the right dose of morphine and then he began to decline rapidly. His doctor came to the room that night and sat with us for nearly two hours. He told me to go home and get some rest, "He'll still be here in the morning." I couldn't bear the thought of him dying alone, but trusted the doctor. I went home and tried to sleep, but couldn't. I kept waiting for a call all night long. When I came back in the morning, the nurses told me he was in what they call Cheyne Stoking; a pattern of breathing that often comes before death. He was unconscious from the morphine and his body was shutting down. I quickly went to his room. He was in a low bed and I sat on the floor beside him. I put his hand in mine, kissed it and told him what a wonderful father he was and how much I loved him. I told him how proud I was of him and that it was okay for him to let go. I told him to go and be with his mama, papa and brother, they were waiting for him, "Papa, don't worry, I will be okay, you can let go." Just then his breathing changed to almost normal, his eyes opened half way and were blazing with electric blue light. I could see him struggling with all his might to open them completely. Slowly he did and looked directly into my eyes. I said, "There you are, I love you papa." A single tear rolled down his cheek. He took a deep breath, let it out slowly, closed his eyes and was gone. I held his hand and sobbed, "Thank you papa, thank you so much." Only love could have brought him out of a morphine coma and ten years of dementia to say goodbye. When I walked in the room, I knew he was already in the light and whole again. He was with his family and friends but had waited for me to get there to say goodbye. He knew how important that would be to me. He left less then three minutes after I arrived. I later asked the doctor, "With all the morphine he was on, what are the chances he would be able to open his eyes, look at me and shed a tear?" His answer was, "It's a miracle." The only explanation is that he was fully aware and conscious of his actions. He was able to keep his physical body breathing and then bring his soul back into it just long enough to show me a miracle and thank me. There will never exist a greater gift of love than this. Thank you papa. Even in the end there was nothing but unconditional love. My father always struggled with life after death. I would often say, "You'll see papa." His eyes told me, "I see Gary, I see."

A couple of days after my father passed away, I was sitting in my backyard crying. I live in the Eastern Hills of San Diego and from my patio I can see Mount Helix standing majestically across the Valley. My gardener once lived in a house right at the top of Mount Helix and I remember visiting her once and watching the hawks soar below from her living room window. As I looked across the valley spotting the very house I visited, I imagined myself living there and how magic it would be. I was just thinking, "I never see hawks here, I want to live in that house so I can be soaring with them." and out of nowhere a large Red Tail Hawk landed in a tree not 30 feet from me and screeched. In seven years of living in my house, I had never seen a hawk in my yard or land in my trees. There are no coincidences. If we are still and in the moment we will clearly see the power of our thoughts as they travel as particles of light through space and create our existence. Miracles and synchronicities happen every day. If we practice being mindful and keep the portal open, we will see their spiritual meaning, lessons and gifts with awakened consciousness. Through the years it has been shown to me that life is a series of events that unfold to teach us how to understand our purpose here. There are endless opportunities to grow, but we need to be present to see them.

Being present is only part of the equation. We have to believe that we are a part of God or more clearly expressed, we are God. I believe this is best explained through the divine message imparted by Jesus Christ and ascended master, St. Germain. In the bible, Exodus 3:14 it talks of the 'I AM' presence as God the omnipotent, omniscient and omnipresent creator of man. The 'I AM' teachings of St. Germain assert we are not only God, but we are able to tap into the creator energy and acquire anything we desire. We are God, the most powerful creator in the universe. We are light, divine love and exist only to eventually learn this.

I have lived my entire life knowing there was something much greater than what was the obvious. A world full of unseen entities, otherworldly beings, gods, gurus and infinite possibilities and paths that lead everyone, eventually to the one thing we are all ultimately looking for, unconditional love. I have shared some amazing stories to illustrate my journey and show you that what I have experienced cannot possibly be coincidence or summed up as "in the realm of possibilities." I have had far too many unexplainable things happen in my life for anyone to convince me otherwise. To me, these events are concrete proof. I can never doubt for one second that there isn't life after this one. Science will always try to find explanations for everything, but science is limited. How would science explain the miracles and gifts in my life? Would they study me and demand that I read everyone's mind with 100% accuracy at all times otherwise say it was just a fluke or a game of odds. Will science chalk up all my experiences as mathematical possibilities?

On the day we released my father's ashes to the sea, I was witness to a true miracle and then, the day after to another that was more beautiful than words can convey. My family and I were in three separate cars on the Oregon coast looking for a private place to put our papa to rest. We proceeded to Haceda Head Lighthouse where there was a small beach where my brother and sister had envisioned us scattering his ashes. When we arrived, the parking lot was full and the beach was crowded with people. Each of us said to ourselves at the same time, "No way!" It was papa telling us that this was not the right place. I believe he was guiding us further up the coast. We eventually found a beautiful secluded beach about ten miles away. We could see from an elevated vantage point on the road that there were less than a handful of people so we pulled off into a small dirt lot and parked. Together the family walked, my sister carrying dad's ashes hugged close to her heart. The walk was a long uneven dirt pathway with small drop-off that led down to the beach. We walked for a couple hundred yards out toward the water and came upon a rock that seemed to appear magically to mark the spot. My mother and brother took a seat on its flat surface. We had a short memorial and the two of them along with my partner, niece and brother-in-law watched as my sister and I carried papa's ashes out to the water. The air temperature and water on the Oregon coast is always very cold but at no time did we feel it as we walked into the waves. We entered up to our waists, opened the bag, placed it in the water and let it fill up. As the sea mixed with the ashes, it created a cloud of light grey which immediately permeated the water all around us. As the ocean drew the water away from the shore, we looked down to see lightening-bolt like streaks pulling the ashes out to sea. We were both crying tears of joy as we said goodbye knowing it was just how he wanted it. He was home. We turned around motioning our fingers and waving our arms to express what we were seeing. When we met the others back at the rock we told them of the magic we witnessed in the water. It was a beautiful experience for everyone.

My partner had taken several photos that day. The next morning while I was looking through them, I came across a picture that showed my sister and me standing side-by-side looking at the waves just after we released my father's ashes. I thought it captured everything perfectly; the beautiful blue sky, the sea and the moment dad was released. It was just how I wanted to remember it. As I examined the photo closer, I began to think, "I wonder if dad left a sign." I zoomed in on my sister and me and as I slowly zoomed out, the sky above us came into view and a word clearly spelled in the clouds jumped out, "LOVE". The discovery was like an explosion of electricity that shot through my body. At first it was hard to comprehend and all I could say was, "Oh my God!" over and over. I took the photo to my partner and asked him to look at the sky and tell me what he saw. He immediately gasped and said, "Oh my God Gary, oh my God, it says LOVE!" This was not only a miracle, it was a miracle that was photographed and videotaped. There were no planes in the sky writing words. There was no editing or Photoshop used. It was our father giving us the greatest gift of our life, a confirmation that he is still with us. To me this was not only proof of an afterlife, but clearly ability for those departed to manipulate the environment after leaving their body. Dad led us that day to the perfect beach with an unmistakable rock to permanently mark his final resting place. He showed us something we will never forget, that love never dies.

My father kept an address list for 70 years in a fireproof box with his most treasured things. Names of people I had never heard of except one, a childhood friend with the name Gregori who he named my brother after. I had memorial cards made and I sent them off all over the world. Two weeks later, I received an email from the son of his childhood friend Gregori whom he had no contact with since the day he left Italy in 1946. His son told me that his father was alive and well and shared many memories of my father and their childhood in Piovenne Rocchette. He went on to say that the most amazing thing was that two days before his father received the memorial card, my father came to him in a dream. My father, not only able to push himself back in his body to say goodbye to me, summon hawks and write love in the sky, was gallivanting in energy all over the world visiting old friends that were forever in his heart.

I see amazing synchronicities and unexplainable phenomena every day because I AM present to recognize it. I physically see the flow of energy particles that make up everything in our infinite existence. They feed me like the air I breathe. I have a direct channel to the Source and while this channel has been open my whole life, it never quite made sense until now. Wisdom is flowing through me at light speed channeled from the collective unconscious of ancient wisdom. This wisdom is in each of us and we are all connected to each other. We are connected to Source. We are God.

I AM living today with an unshakable belief in the energy love and magical world of the unseen. For my father loved us so much he wrote love across the sky. He lives in me and all I need to do is think of him and he is here filling my heart with so much love that it spills over from my eyes.

"Nothing is moving only you. Be still and know that I AM."

One morning while deep in meditation vibrating with particles of light around me, I had an incredible realization. Even though I felt the vibrations and could see the particles of light dancing around and through me, my body was perfectly still within it. I decided to lift my arms and move my hands through the space in front of me. I realized that the only thing moving was my hands and everything else was still. Here in this stillness I was moving about like an astronaut weightless hopping across the surface of the moon. I could see clearly that I was moving through a beautifully still universe of sparkling light, living golden warmth of unconditional love. When St. Germain says in the *I AM Discourses*, I AM the resurrection and the life, I believe he meant that from energy, we are created and projected into the vast matrix of life like images projected onto a movie screen. We are resurrection from particles of light. My arms moved through the infinite light, my breath taking in the same particles that have existed throughout eternity. I inhaled countless souls whom traveled through my body coexisting with me yet within a universe of their own. The separation of my body from the energy I was moving through helped me to see clearer that from sensory overload created by our human bodies we are separated from our natural bodiless state of oneness with Source, Source that is entirely still golden light and unconditional love. It was here in this light my father wrote love in the sky, separated from his human body, but resurrected as Source.

"Love unconditionally. When you judge, you are judging yourself for we are all one."

Remember when we open our mouths to speak badly about someone, whatever judgment we have is how we feel about ourselves and has nothing to do with the other person. We must learn to accept everyone for who they are. We do not know their path or pain. Learn to love yourself for it is the greatest thing you can do for others. When we love ourselves, then we will stop judging others.

"You may be the spark that changes the life of another human being, but each person is the creator of his or her own existence."

I have learned that while we may be the spark that changes the life of another, ultimately we cannot stop their karma. We can only change our own. We may offer advice, council, coach and plant seeds, but ultimately it is the volition of the person. I think of how many times signs are ignored and their miraculous impact minimized or scoffed at. You can lead a horse to water, but you cannot make them drink. I think of the addict. We may think our advice is helping when in reality it could be hurting. People learn on their own time, they have to experience their fate in its full intent before karma is erased. We cannot live our lives based on others experiences, it is our path and ours alone. If it were not you that guided someone then it would be someone else, if not in this lifetime, another. Telling someone what he or she needs to do is as successful as not. It can seem convoluted and confusing, but a simple takeaway is for each of us to be a non-judgmental support to everyone. Share your experiences, but don't offer advice and if from sharing it helps to change someone's life then the timing was right, the alignment in place and the lesson revealed. Whether or not someone is ready is unknown.

"I AM divine energy melding ancient wisdom into the DNA of this life structure."

The energy signature of unconditional love is deeply embedded into our DNA. As our heart beats oxygenated blood throughout our bodies, it not only brings life to the structure, but also carries nutrients from the Source. In this river of living, vibrating golden light is pure unconditional love permeating every cell of energy in our existence. I

AM the nucleus of all things and through me all things can happen. I AM the connecting thought that brings the realization. I AM unconditional love that seeks only itself. I AM the touch of my mother, heart of an angel and breath of my father. I AM that I AM.

"Find comfort in love and make yourself at home."

Unless we are ready and able to live a life entirely devoted to meditation and spiritual growth, we are left to live in world of the senses. There are many monks in Tibet, devotees in India and others around the world living in silent meditation in the final preparation for ascension of the soul to another dimension. If we are not yet ready, and few are, we are left to live in a world of people, jobs, news, television, wars, Internet and the cosmic delusion. If we are not yet ready to take the final steps of ascension, then we are still here to learn lessons from life. I spend a lot of time in my work learning about the latest research on successful aging. The universities talk about essential elements of diet, exercise, socialization, spirituality and the list goes on. I've been to conferences about it and no matter what our age is, we continue to search for meaning in life. We try to live as long and as healthy as possible. Most of us are somewhat in denial of our mortality. No matter what our age, we are aging. I often see seniors looking for that magic elixir that will slow the aging process while spending hours at doctors trying to feel better. The latest research shows that the less our intestines work, the longer we will live. We don't need to exercise that much and something as standing for 20 minutes a day is just as effective as hitting the gym. People wanting and striving to live forever when the reality is we do. Life is a comedy, a tragedy, a quest, and a giant cosmic delusion. Find solace in knowing that while in this body, home is the space in which we live. If we live in place full of negativity, defensiveness, struggle and pain, then we will not find comfort there. Go deep within to find the Source of unconditional love. If we live here, we will find comfort and home wherever we go.

"You must always be kind to people; remember when you are kind to others you are being kind to yourself."

There are two ways a bad situation can go, worse or better. We pick. No matter what the situation, if we are kind and loving it's going to go better. The important thing to remember is to be in the moment. Stop, pause and play out the tape before we react. If we do this one thing, it will change our lives, the outcome of any situation and save us from a lot of struggle. I was talking with a co-worker who is remarrying his wife after previously divorcing. I have seen this happen several times in my life, giving love a second chance. As we began to discuss what went wrong and the challenges, a pattern began to emerge, everyone sweats the small stuff. The majority of their angst came from simple things such as picking out a sink or how towels are hung in the bathroom. Inevitably these small things became bickering, a fight, a blow out and then resentment. Once this happens, guess what? There goes intimacy and your whole evening, week or worse. After a while, these resentments build up and we can barely stand the person let alone want any sort of intimacy with him or her.

What if in every situation that is irritating us, we are mindful to play out the tape. One, how important is this really and two, is it more important than what the aftermath will be? Take a situation such as our spouses coming home from work every night, taking off their shoes and socks, leaving them on the living room floor. We have admonished him or her countless times for this same issue and still they don't seem to care. We trip over the shoes one last time before the fireworks start. We become angry and yell, "Why don't you put your damn shoes away!" You brought home a wonderful dinner to share and now you can barely stand to sit in front of each other and eat. There is no conversation, only blank stares, resentment and hurt feelings. At the end of the day as the tape plays out we should ask ourselves, was it worth getting mad about and ruining an entire dinner and evening not to mention any chances of romance or intimacy? First, the shoes on the floor are not the problem; this is where it goes wrong every time. If they don't have a problem with taking off their shoes when they get home and leaving them on the living room floor then it's not their problem it is ours. We can't change someone and we shouldn't try. If we have a problem with it, how hard is it to pick them up and put them away ourselves? This single yet easy thing could save an entire evening and even a relationship. We feel better they are not on the floor and the night goes on as planned. We laugh over dinner, snuggle on the coach and have passionate sex later that night. Imagine this tape playing out in all our small stuff such as: whiskers in the sink, dishes on the counter and lowering the lid on the toilet seat. Remember it's small stuff. If it bothers you, do something about it. It is your problem after all. Play the tape out even further. What if on the way home that night, your spouse is killed in a tragic car accident? I can assure you that you would miss those shoes on the floor, dishes on the counter and whiskers in the sink and wish that every day you could have them back and you would clean them up with love in your heart. Do nice things for others. It is the most important thing we can do. Never be angry, move fluid through the drama and stay kind and loving. Live each day with strength of character and know you are making a difference.

"I AM able to manipulate the landscape through which I move."

We have the ability to create every moment of our existence. While we can't always control everything that comes our way, our creation unfolds as we react. We go to a restaurant, sit and wait for 30 minutes and nobody acknowledges us, we get upset and start looking around. We see that the place is full and there are only two people serving tables. We get more upset and want to leave. We're hungry and in a hurry. This is unacceptable we say to ourselves. The waiter comes and seems to have an attitude, ours is worse and the situation spirals into a horrible evening and the food isn't that great either. Everyone around us looks unhappy as well. All around, we have created a horrible experience. Yes, we have created it. If we shift our perception of what is going on, we find that there is more to the story. There are only three restaurants in town. They are all full because there are 2000 people at a conference down the street. The waiters have been working over-time with non-stop crowds all day. We are one of dozens of customers to come through the door that day all with the same attitude. Remember, we are the most powerful creator in our universe. Our creation can go another way. We go to a restaurant, sit for 30 minutes and instead of looking around for someone to take our order, we take the time to reflect on our day and have a good conversation with our friends. We are enjoying our conversation when the waiter comes 30 minutes later to take our order. We notice that they seem tense; we know it has nothing to do with us so we smile and ask, "How are you doing today?" They express how busy it's been and how many hours they have been on their feet and we apologize and say, "I'm sorry. I wish you could sit down and take a break!" They appreciate that we've taken time to acknowledge them as a human. They take our order and we smile and thank them. They have a little more spring in their step when they leave. Each time they walk by you smile. We give them a heartfelt thank you each time they drop off something at the table and we look them in the eyes. We tell them how good the food is and thank them again. Our service gets better and we find them going out of their way to make sure our experience is a good one. Since our spirits are good, the food tastes better and we leave having had a good experience. The creation is ours, the choice is clear. Remember there is neither good nor bad, there simply is. Move through the scene as observer and know we are not the scene, we are the creator.

"Transcend and believe there is no force greater than you in the universe."

We are not just a creator in the matrix, we are co-creator with others. Together we bring a mix of reactions and movements within the landscape. The two scenarios at the restaurant illustrate the power we have to manipulate the landscape through our perception and actions by playing out the tape with the end result being positive. I can't say it enough. Find the good in everything, be grateful to have a meal, be grateful that you can afford to go out, be kind to everyone. If you can't afford to go out, be grateful that you are alive and healthy. Find beauty in nature, it's free. There is beauty everywhere around us. We have to choose to see it. We must always try to surround ourselves with people who are grateful, kind and loving. I watched a special on television fundraising for education of children in Africa. Even though many were homeless and hungry, they didn't see themselves that way. Most interviewed were happy, grateful and hopeful. They had dreams, but were not tainted or discouraged by their existence. We are all born into this life with a purpose and a path. Be grateful no matter what yours is.

"There is no construct of time and place in the infinite. There is simply everything at once."

In the infinite universe there are principles that we cannot understand within the constructs of science. Even the most advanced technology and scientific theories cannot factually explain the vastness of our universe or the ability to break a molecule into smaller and smaller particles. Where does it all end in space and the smallest realms of the molecular? I call it the omnipotent infinite or the immeasurable energy of God. In the matrix, which is the place where all exists both in thought and physicality, everything is happening at the same time. There are multiple dimensions where our energy lives simultaneously. We are limitless in our existence. We interpret everything as what we can see with our human eyes. We are not tuned into the frequencies or vibrations that allow us to see it. It is sort of like looking at the propeller of an airplane flying through the sky, it is not visible as it's spinning so fast, it is invisible to the naked eye however, when taking a photo of it while looking at your iPhone screen, you can see the propeller moving in almost slow motion. The camera allows you to see a different reality because it measures the movement of objects at a different speed by slowing down or looking at pixels of light rows in a way that the human eye cannot compute or see. So it is the same with alternate realities and other dimensions. If our eyes were a camera that could tune to the right wavelength or speed, it could possibly pick up something we ordinarily couldn't see such as inter-dimensional beings or the propeller spinning on an aircraft. I attended a conference called "Contact in the Desert". There was a wide range of speakers from self-help gurus to ancient alien theorists. There were speakers who claim to have been abducted by aliens and continue to be to this day. Many tell a story of fear and survival, being a "victim" while others tell a story of signing contracts with otherworldly beings with an understanding that they are here to bring a message to the masses. The most striking thing about the conference was how many different theories and possibilities exist. There was a sense of love, understanding and openness amongst everyone. The message was clear. Never stop questioning and pursuing the truth.

"I AM Alien, Man, God, Love."

I love coffee. It's one way that I treat myself every day. I learned to love it as a young child. Growing up with an Italian grandmother whose only words in English were, "I love you very much" "You are a very good boy" and "very delicious", I learned the language of love by sitting with her in the morning and watching her make us café latte. She had one of those old-fashioned metal pots where you put the ground espresso in the bottom and the water in the top, let it boil and get perfect espresso every time. She would take the coffee, pour it into a pan with whole milk and sugar then bring it to a boil. It was divine. She would serve it with Stella D'oro Italian cookies. The ritual was the same every time. Cookie goes in the coffee for just a second then in your mouth before it dissolved in the coffee. We would sit and enjoy it together and the shared smiles between bites and sips were priceless. My heart overflows with love thinking about it. Each time as we got to the end of the cup, she would get us spoons so we could relish the remnants of the cookies at the bottom and when finished she would say, "very delicious".

Each morning, I wake, open my eyes and acknowledge I AM alive. I slowly stretch the muscles of my body that have become tight during the night drawing breath in and out to a count of seven. Once I feel ready I slowly sit up, grab my headphones from the nightstand, place my feet on the floor and stand. I complete my morning routine then head to the kitchen to make my coffee. I AM grateful our coffee maker brews a pot in three minutes. Once brewed, I add the milk and sugar the way that my nonna did and head to my favorite chair to begin my meditation.

My meditation is a three-step process, affirmation, manifestation and connection. I place the headphones on my head, turn on the noise canceling feature, start my favorite meditation music which is the I AM meditation by

Wayne Dyer and begin with my affirmations. I AM God, I AM love, I AM happy, I AM healthy, I AM the resurrection and the life. I immediately begin to feel peace and joy in my heart. I AM in full awareness of the God I AM and connected to Source. I then begin to visualize what I want to manifest in my life. I imagine what it is, how it looks, feels and the outcome. In manifestation, it is very important to kick your imagination into hyper drive. For example, if you want a certain job you have to create the entire scene. Think about where the headquarters for this job is. Look it up online or drive by it so you can visualize driving there every day. See yourself getting out of bed, getting ready, getting in your car driving the exact route, parking, getting out of your car, walking to the entrance of the building, entering, walking to your office, saying hello to people, getting to your desk, sitting down, and starting your routine. You have to be specific in your visualization. You have to play it like a movie down to the minutest details. Feeling what it is like to sit at your desk, touching the phone and keyboard of your computer, specifics of what you will be doing. Visualize the players you will be working with, how you will interact, looking at your bank account on payday and seeing the deposit from the company there. Everything you can imagine about it, make it real, as if it is already happening, like you have been doing it for years. This is the amount of focus you must have when being creator and manifesting. You can never falter in your vision and never have doubts, the minute you do you tear apart your creation. The moment a negative thought comes, laugh, trash it and replace with what you want. This will take practice, but no matter what it is you are trying to manifest, you must use this focus and attention to detail.

Another example would be the car you are driving to the office. If you have a dream car, actually study photos of it or go to the dealer and sit in one so you know what it looks and feels like, test drive it so when you are visualizing driving it you actually know how it is to do so. See yourself driving it, placing your body in the seat, gripping the wheel, putting it in drive, turning on the stereo, setting up your blue tooth, admiring the color and acceleration, feeling the bumps on the road, maneuvering traffic, again, play it like a movie. These are only examples of manifesting. You must be steadfast in this and do it every day and do not give up. The day you stop the lower your chances of success will be. Each day you do it the visualizations become easier until it is a memory of how it really is and it flows naturally. You will no longer have to imagine it, it is automatically there and you are doing it.

Once I AM done visualizing, I think about the people I want in my life. There are those who are already there that I spend less time on and those who are not, I spend more. I imagine us face to face, talking; I kiss their forehead and send unconditional love from my heart chakra to theirs. I see us sitting in my living room discussing specific topics and making dinner in the kitchen, eating meals and sharing life experiences. I see their faces, the feel of their hugs, the smell of their hair, the tone of their voice and eye contact, laughing and living in each other's lives. For the people already in my life, I picture his or her face, hug them and send them unconditional love. Those who are not and I would like in my life I spend more time with specific events that will lead to our friendship. After this, I think about where I want to live, what I want my day-to-day life to be. I get extremely specific about where my house will be, what it will look like, I build it from the ground up and get into the minutest details from wiring speakers to faucets in the sink. I build each room one by one and create the vision with the most intricate details including touching the sheets on the bed. The more specific you get, the better. You have to actually be living in the space, touching the surfaces, feeling the walls, showering in the shower, swimming in the pool, cooking in the kitchen, doing laundry, opening the windows, listening to the way rain sounds when it hits the roof, talking on the phone while sitting on the sofa, holding a pillow in your lap, eating at the dining room table with the people you want in your life. It needs to play like a movie.

Once I have made my affirmations, created my world of people, my dream job, house and life, I go deeper to the Source of where all creation is manifested. Conscious contact with my God self. I begin by going back to my affirmations and become one with the I AM presence. When I close my eyes, there directly in front of me are particles of light in varying colors, shades and vibration. It is there for everyone. You just need to close your eyes and see the dancing energy unfold before you. Concentrate on this energy and begin to see that this very energy is what is vibrating through your entire body. It is everywhere in the universe, not just before your closed eyes. It is the spark of interconnected lights that make up the entirety of your existence. If you have trouble seeing the light or vibrating molecules, close your eyes as tight as you can and you will begin to see a myriad of things happen, sometimes it will look like snow on an unreceptive television set and other times like blocks of pixels on a distorted computer screen. The more you press your eyes tightly the more you will begin to see these variations. This technique is only to get you to see the energy. Once you see it, relax your eyes and you will then be able to identify the specks of light vibrating before you. This is Source energy. It is the battery of your existence. Without it, there is no life. Take these particles of light and imagine them vibrating in every particle within the universe of your body. You can program these vibrations with whatever energy you chose. Being God creator you can pull unconditional love, feel it, hold it and charge the particles of light with this vibration. Send it into every infinite space within your body and then outward to the space around you. Send it to other people. Keep vibrating it out into the air, space, time, the cosmos, through black holes, galaxies and as far out as you can imagine. Let it become infinite. Once you are vibrating at infinite speed, you are basking in Source energy. Fill the space with unconditional love. You have learned what that is, tears falling, heart swelling, unconditional acceptance, peace, pure light, energy swilling in a pool of warm, golden light that is fluid and perfect like floating in a bath of warm water. I stay there as long as possible sending unconditional love through my body to every corner of its universe. In my universe, there is peace, no wars, only unconditional love, everything lives within a realm of living golden light and only goodness is allowed. I AM the ruler of my universe, God the most powerful creator. From the light I see my nonna's face appear and she reaches out to take my hand, it's time. I reach down to the ledge, pick up my coffee and take my first sip. I hear her say, "Very delicious!" I close my eyes and repeat, I will take this love with me, I will move fluid through the day and not be affected by negativity, I will watch and remain calm and loving no matter what. I place my hand on my heart chakra and rub it left to right and repeat, "I AM love, I AM forgiving, I AM grateful, I AM not this body, I AM divine love."

The Miracle of Padre Pio

During a recent visit to Los Angeles I spent the evening with my favorite aunt and we talked deeply about God and spirituality. I shared with her the memory of my uncle's relic of Padre Pio's blood-stained cloth and how it had called to me my whole life. I knew that this relic had a very high vibration and with it the physical real life imprint of the miracle. It was long after my last visual of this relic in the early 90s that Padre Pio was canonized a saint by the Catholic Church. During a break in our conversation, my aunt went into her bedroom and came out with the piece of cloth clutched in her hand. It was displayed just how I remembered it in my youth encased in a jewel encrusted circular frame on a brass stand. Immediately I was overwhelmed. I told her how much that memory meant to me. Without hesitation she gave me the relic to keep. I was overcome with emotion and felt such deep gratitude for her trust in me to have it. I held it like it was the most precious thing on earth and brought it home to its resting place on the ledge above the headboard of my bed. I started adding Padre Pio to each day's meditation swimming in the energy of his light.

Not long after my father passed away, I sent out memorial cards around the globe and it was several months later that I received a handwritten card from a cousin named Horacio in Germany. I had never met him, but my father and his mother Katarina were first cousins and knew each other as children in Argentina during the late 20s and early 30s. After my father retired, he visited Katarina in Buenos Aires several times. He reconnected with the family and Horacio was her oldest son who later moved to Germany with his wife. My father had visited him in Germany during the late 80s. The card came with a photo of my father, grandmother and grandfather at the family villa in Capilla del Monte, Argentina. He wrote that his mother had passed away several months before my father and at the end she expressed to him how important it was to stay in touch with the family. I had wanted to write him back immediately, but time and commitments kept me from doing so. Steve reminded me on a weekly basis, "You really need to respond to your cousin." I misplaced the envelope with the return address and couldn't find it for months and couldn't find the address list I used to send it in the first place. I tried researching his name on line to find a Facebook account or some other way to contact him, but to no avail. I once had his email address, but hadn't used it for close to eight years and since had deleted all my contacts with upgrades to my computers and devices over time and it was gone. I did finally find the envelope with the return address, but it was not written clearly and had a German address that was hard to read. I researched the address online but couldn't confirm it was his. I had pretty much given up on sending a return card.

On July 16th 2016, I started my day with my usual routine as described in the whisper *I AM Alien, Man, God Love*. This day I was vibrating in the light unlike anything I have experienced to date. I felt overwhelmed by the love I was feeling not only from the Masters but also from Padre Pio and my father. I was so grateful that tears were spilling from my eyes. I sensed the energy of my father all around me, my body was energized and I had goose bumps and my hair was standing straight up. I could feel the sensation of my father caressing the back of my head with a gentle touch of love and kindness. I sat bathing in the love and began speaking out loud, "Thank you papa, thank you so much." I had my noise cancelling headphones on, listening to Wayne Dyer's *I AM Wishes Fulfilled Mediation* on my iPhone which I had placed on Airplane Mode. I was not wearing my contact lenses and without them, everything is very blurry. As I opened my eyes, tears still spilling from them, I looked up in the tree above me and there were dozens of birds looking down. I knew instantly this was my family and loved ones. This filled me with more energy, love and tears. I suddenly realized that without any contacts or correction to my vision, I could see perfectly. The outline of each leaf on every branch, every bird, even their tiny eyes staring down at me was perfectly clear. I simply could not believe what I was seeing and instantly realized I was experiencing a miracle. I thanked my father and Padre Pio and felt strongly that they both were present.

As I pulled the ear buds from my ears, I realized that the caressing that I felt on the back of my head was humming birds literally flying and poking the back of my head and the sensation I felt was their wings fluttering in my hair as they flew around me. I sat stunned as the tears spilled from my eyes as the gratitude was overwhelming. I soaked in the love and grace until all was still and I realized I had just experienced something so amazing that words could never express the magnitude.

Slowly my vision became blurry and I could no longer see the details in the tree and the birds flew away. As I gathered my thoughts, I turned my phone off of Airplane Mode and an email popped up as a banner across my screen. It was from my father. It said email from: Lucian. I couldn't believe my eyes, how could this be? I quickly opened it up and along with it being sent to me, it had the email addresses to every single one of my family members including my cousin Horacio in Germany. Mind you, my father had dementia for nearly a decade so I had not received an email from him for over eight years. This email came from an unknown email address Lucian@sepientiasiculorum.ro. The only email address he ever had was the one I created for him in the early 90s and this wasn't it. I knew that it had to be a spam email, but how did it have all my family's emails? How did it come as the first email to me after this miracle I just experienced? The only thing in the message of the body was, http://superb.universaltronics.com/Lucian and then signed, Lucian. The link was dead. If my father writing the word love in the clouds as we released his ashes into the sea wasn't enough, this was further proof of his existence as living energy.

I sent emails to the family and fulfilled my father and Katarina's wishes for us to keep in touch. I researched the email address and came to a dead end. The most I could tell is that the email address was hosted by a university in Hungary. I researched the words "sepientia siculorum" and they are Latin for knowledgeable Italian or (Sicilian). Interesting that I would witness a miracle then receive an email from my Italian father at an email address meaning knowledgeable Italian and a link to the Superb Universe! The only avenue I could find online for the link took me in a round about way to a site selling antique sterling silver communion sets. Padre Pio, Papa, Miracles? Indeed.

I AM grateful for the blessings and signs I receive.

I AM one with all I love. All my deceased friends and loved ones surround me, tears spill from my eyes with the most tender and beautiful, pure and comforting energy of unconditional love. I AM that, I AM energy.

Two Years Later

I have witnessed the miraculous power of manifestation over and over, but nothing tops what I'm about to tell you. It was after two solid years of meditating every day about living in Maui surrounded by highly evolved spiritual people that I received a message from Sufian Chaudhary telling me that he was moving there. I was simply stunned, then ecstatic at the success of my creation. I immediately knew that I would be following him soon, for how could I have manifested Sufian travel half-way around the world to live in the very place that I envisioned for two years, if I wasn't going to be there as well? In September of 2016, my partner Steve and I boarded a plane for Maui to meet Sufian in person. He had moved there a couple of days before our arrival and the excitement was building. I had rented a cabana on the beach in front of the Sheraton Maui over-looking Black Rock. We had been texting all day and finally Sufian and his girlfriend were driving from the other side of the island to meet us. I gave him directions to the exact spot of our cabana. When we first embraced, it was like two brothers reunited after decades of being apart; ancient souls reunited for the first time in this life. We had developed an on-line relationship over the past two years and to finally meet in person was miraculous. Sufian and I swam out from shore about 100 yards and looked back at the West Maui Mountains and the Sheraton in the distance. I had never shared with Sufian that I had been meditating his living in Maui for the past two years. Nor did I share that I had a photo of him and the Maui shoreline on the wish board framed by my bedside. But as we swam side by side, I shared it all. We looked back at the Sheraton Maui in the distance and I pointed to the very room where I had finished his book *World of Archangels* and shared the confirmation dream with Steve. Interestingly enough, on this trip, we were staying in the room right next door. As Sufian and I slowly floated further from shore, we soaked in the sun and shared in the miracle of our meeting again in this lifetime. We both agreed that my destiny lay in Maui and that I wouldn't be far behind him.

I know with certainty that the greatest miracles of this life still lay ahead of me in Hawaii, but I am grateful, amazed and stunned at the outcome of this incredible journey to date. The foundation for the light bridge has been set. I AM excited for the whispers and miracles still to come and look forward to sharing them when they do.

Gary
January 8, 2017

Printed in the United States
By Bookmasters

.